Read Write Inc.

Handbook

Series developed by Ruth Miskin

Written by Janey Pursglove and Jenny Roberts

Spelling consultant: Jennifer Chew

Contents

Overview 2
   - What is *Read Write Inc. Spelling*? 2
   - When should children use *Read Write Inc. Spelling*? 2
   - What training is provided? 2
   - Online training films 3
   - Why is it important to have a systematic spelling programme? 3
Read Write Inc. Spelling resources 4
   - Extra Practice Zone 10
How does the programme work? 12
   - Route through *Read Write Inc. Spelling* for Year 2/Primary 3 12
   - Route through *Read Write Inc. Spelling* for Years 3–6/Primary 4–7 ... 13
   - Timetables 14
Planning 15
   - Example plans for *Read Write Inc. Spelling* 15
Yearly timings for *Read Write Inc. Spelling* 16
   - Additional spelling sessions 17
Pre-programme activities for assessment and revision of Year 1/Primary 2
    phonics and spelling 18
How a unit works 23
Classroom management 34
Terminology and progression 40
Activities for teaching Red and Orange words 41
Read Write Inc. Spelling content matched to National Curriculum
    English Appendix 1: Spelling 44
Assessment in *Read Write Inc. Spelling* 51
   - The statutory end of Key Stage tests 54
Coverage linked to the curricula in England, Scotland, Wales
    and Northern Ireland 55
Overview of activities on the Extra Practice Zone 63

OXFORD
UNIVERSITY PRESS

Overview

What is *Read Write Inc. Spelling*?

Read Write Inc. Spelling is a robust, fast-paced, systematic spelling programme for children in Years 2–6 (Primary 3–7). It has proved itself to be an effective and popular programme in schools nationwide. The programme gives all the support and resources you need to teach the spelling component of the National Curriculum in England with confidence and clarity to ensure that children:

> 'spell new words correctly and have plenty of practice in spelling them … including exception words and homophones'

> 'spell words as accurately as possible using their phonic knowledge and other knowledge of spelling, such as morphology [the study of the form of words] and etymology [the study of the origins and development of words]'

> 'are supported in understanding and applying the concepts of word structure'

> 'spell words that they have not yet been taught by using what they have learnt about how spelling works in English'

When should children use *Read Write Inc. Spelling*?

This spelling programme is for children in Year 2/P3 and above who have completed *Read Write Inc. Phonics* (the spelling programme can be taught alongside the Phonics programme from Grey level) or for children who have not used *Read Write Inc. Phonics* and can read fluently.

Ideally, *Read Write Inc. Spelling* should be used alongside *Read Write Inc. Comprehension* and *Literacy and Language*. However, it can also be used successfully alone, or alongside other literacy programmes, as long as children have the necessary phonic knowledge gained from other programmes.

In order to assess or revise children's knowledge and skills before embarking on *Read Write Inc. Spelling*, lead the children through the pre-programme activities on pp. 18–22.

What training is provided?

Online training is provided by Ruth Miskin Training (RMT).

The online training offers 20 videos providing step-by-step guidance for all the activities in the *Read Write Inc. Spelling* programme.

The online spelling training is included in the RMT Online Training Subscription. It can also be purchased separately.

Go to www.ruthmiskin.com to find out more.

Overview

Online training films

In this handbook, there are references to the RMT training films for *Read Write Inc. Spelling*, indicated by this film symbol:

Where there is a film symbol, there is a training film relevant to the section, providing further guidance and support.

Please note: The training films are on the RMT Online Training Subscription, whereas the Spelling zone videos, which explain spelling rules to the children, are on the *Read Write Inc. Spelling* Online Resource on Oxford Owl for School.

Why is it important to have a systematic spelling programme?

The English language has one of the richest vocabularies in the world. For more than 1000 years, the English language has inherited and assimilated many words from other languages: Latin, French, Greek and German. We have also kept aspects of the spellings of these words, which has created the most complex alphabetic language in the world.

German, Italian, Spanish, Finnish, Polish, Greek and Welsh children learn to read and spell quickly because their speech sounds are written down, more or less, the same way in every word – i.e. they have a simple alphabetic code. This means that once they have cracked the code they can write any word correctly.

English, however, has many ways of writing each sound because we have more speech sounds than letters. For example, we write the sound *ay* at least eight ways: pl**ay**, r**ai**n, m**a**ke, **eigh**t, str**aigh**t, r**eig**n, r**ein**, br**ea**k. This means that the alphabetic code is very complex and takes a long time to learn.

Read Write Inc. Spelling is a programme based on the understanding that we do have a sound-based writing system, albeit a very complex one. Everyone uses the same 44 sounds to *speak* all English words, though the way we *write down* these sounds varies. (The 44 sounds differ a little, depending on accent.) So one of the keys to good spelling is to remember how to spell these sounds in different words – and this does not happen overnight. Even now, as adults, we tend to avoid writing down words that we cannot spell.

Just as a quick test, which of the words below are spelt incorrectly?

> supacede   brocolli   aparent   consede   proceede   idiosincracy   concensus   accomodate
> rhythm   optholmologist   diptheria   anomoly   caesaerean   grafitti   diaharrioah

Spelling tends to improve throughout our lives and it is only with lots of practice that we become good spellers. (By the way, none of the words above are spelt correctly.)

Traditionally, the teaching of spelling has often been arduous, painstaking and, sadly, boring. The practice of a weekly Friday spelling test had mixed results, with some children getting spellings right on the day, but forgetting them just hours later, and other children simply getting them wrong and becoming demoralized.

The process of learning to spell is cumulative for most children. Only a few lucky children learn to spell effortlessly without structured teaching. Most need explicit systematic teaching that is continually practised and reinforced, until spelling knowledge is committed to children's long-term memory. The *Read Write Inc. Spelling* programme provides this structured, systematic teaching.

Read Write Inc. Spelling resources

Read Write Inc. Spelling resources are structured to reflect the requirements of the National Curriculum in England. We have divided the content into separate years in the programme to suggest a logical teaching sequence of all required topics by the end of Key Stage 2/Primary 7.

The basic structure of *Read Write Inc. Spelling*, in terms of resources, is outlined below.

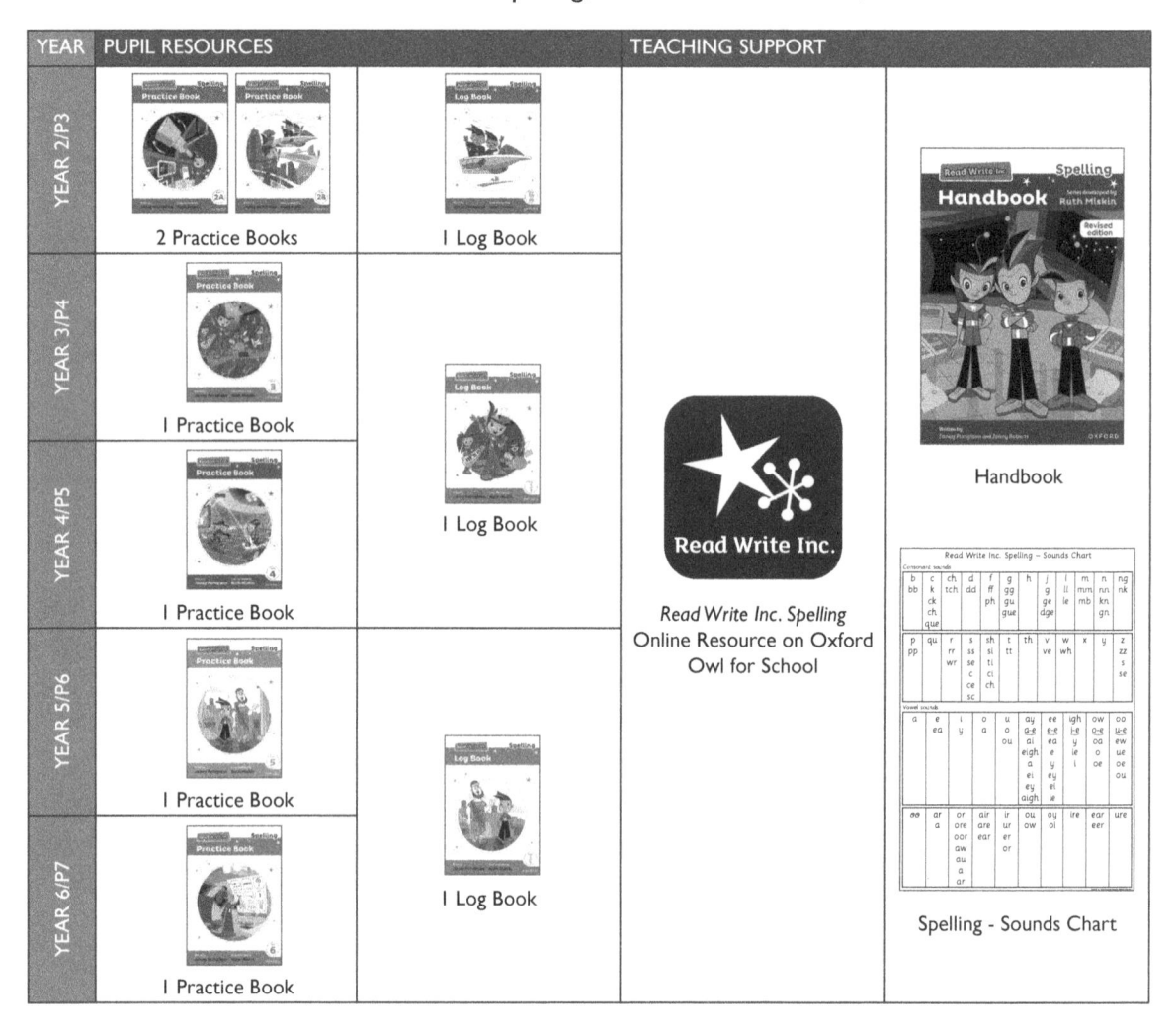

YEAR	PUPIL RESOURCES		TEACHING SUPPORT	
YEAR 2/P3	2 Practice Books	1 Log Book	*Read Write Inc. Spelling* Online Resource on Oxford Owl for School	Handbook
YEAR 3/P4	1 Practice Book	1 Log Book		
YEAR 4/P5	1 Practice Book			
YEAR 5/P6	1 Practice Book	1 Log Book		Spelling - Sounds Chart
YEAR 6/P7	1 Practice Book	1 Log Book		

The **Handbook** guides you through the programme, summarizing the teaching scope and offering support and advice on how best to implement *Read Write Inc. Spelling*, including blueprint lesson plans, timetables and curriculum matching charts.

The **Practice Books** contain partner, group and independent activities to consolidate understanding and to practise and monitor children's spelling. *Practice Book 2A* also contains a short section of pre-programme activities for children to complete, under teacher guidance, for revision and assessment of Year 1/P2 phonics and spelling before embarking on the full *Read Write Inc. Spelling* programme.

Spelling Log Books enable children to record their own words to revise and give opportunity for on-going self-assessment. Children are encouraged to take these home to share with parents, carers or older siblings who can help children to practise spelling their weekly selection of words. The Spelling Log Books also contain a glossary of key spelling terms and a chart of Red or Orange words.

Online Resource on Oxford Owl for School

The **Online Resource** on Oxford Owl for School is used for whole-class teaching.

A quick video walk-through of the Online Resource can be accessed through the hyperlinked Overview document. This is the first document listed on the Online Resource.

All online files and Spelling zone videos can be accessed through the Overview document.

Three animated alien characters from the Spelling Planet introduce and explain the spelling focus for each unit. (See p.6 for more detail about the Spelling zone videos.)

Other online files on the Online Resource include:

✫ A digital version of the pre-programme activities from *Practice Book 2A*, to revise and assess children's identification of basic speech sounds and the alphabetic code for late starters, and to assess and consolidate understanding of key spelling patterns taught in Year 1/P2. There are also pre-programme special focus pages online which can be used to consolidate children's knowledge of key concepts from Year 1 of the National Curriculum in England. See pp.51–54 for more information about assessment, including Year 1.

Read Write Inc. Spelling resources

- ✯ Six Practice tests per year group, plus two Practice tests for Year 1/P2 and six challenge Practice tests for Year 6/P7. An assessment spreadsheet is also available to enable you to track children's progress through the tests and identify which concepts the class may need to consolidate.

- ✯ Printable versions of the Spelling zone video scripts.

- ✯ Display files with answers to Dots and dashes, Word changers and Choose the right word to allow you to discuss the answers with the class.

- ✯ Word banks. These are editable files with six words per A4 sheet, so they can be cut up and displayed. The Word banks consist of:
  - words from individual units
  - Red words (words specified in the National Curriculum as 'common exception words' in Years 1 and 2, plus some additional high frequency words with an unusual spelling).
  - Orange words (words specified in the National Curriculum word lists for Years 3/4 and Years 5/6).

- ✯ Consolidation sessions as an optional extra if your children need further practice to reinforce what they have learnt in each unit.

- ✯ Special focus pages (and answers) from the Practice Books for whole-class display.

- ✯ Extra Challenge dictation sentences and More challenge dictation sentences for fast finishers.

- ✯ A printable version of the *Read Write Inc. Spelling* – Sounds Chart to display in classrooms.

- ✯ Extra Practice Zone with more than 1000 activity pages, providing further practice and consolidation for faster progress. See p.10 for further information.

Spelling zone

At the start of each unit in *Read Write Inc. Spelling*, there is a video in which a character from the Spelling Planet introduces and explains the key concept for the unit. This is called the Spelling zone video and it is the first file on the Online Resource for each unit, e.g. File 2.1. There is also a printable version of the video script for each unit on the Online Resource.

The Spelling zone is a space station that floats above the Spelling Planet.

Introducing the Spelling Team

The Spelling Team characters are Star Spellers called Zeta, Gamma and Mu. They are 'humaliens' whose mission is to help Earth children become confident spellers. They are very interested in all things related to spelling and are keen to share their enthusiasm with Earth children!

The characters present spelling concepts in a carefully levelled and engaging way. Using your video controls, you can pace the progress of the explanations and revisit key sections if you wish, to ensure all children get a good grounding in the spelling rule or concept being explored.

The Spelling Team characters are confident spellers but they find some aspects of English spelling puzzling or unexpected. They flag up Tips and Weird Word Warnings to help children get to grips with rules and exceptions, and highlight points of interest to help children complete the activities correctly.

Read Write Inc. Spelling resources

Zeta   Gamma   Mu

There are two versions of the Spelling Team. The younger characters 'regenerate' as older versions in Years 4, 5 and 6/P5, 6 and 7.

Zeta   Gamma   Mu

7

Read Write Inc. Spelling resources

Each Star Speller from the Spelling Team has particular areas of interest:

Gamma loves sport so his explanations are often related to his recent Zoneball matches or sporting adventures.

Zeta enjoys music and singing, so she will often share rhymes or jingles in her videos. Like Gamma, Zeta loves playing Zoneball, too.

Mu is an adventurer, historian, time traveller, code-breaker and archaeologist. If a spelling focus is related to the history and etymology of a word, he might travel back in time to find out more about it.

Link to the Spelling zone in the Practice Books

After watching the Spelling zone video, children complete the Spelling zone section of their Practice Book for the unit, which includes a quick recap of key information, plus a variety of partner activities to practise key rules and patterns.

Year 6/P7 Spelling zone

In Year 6/P7, the structure of the Spelling zone is slightly different. The teaching in this year revises all the key concepts explored in earlier years. The characters progress to the Presidential Suite, where there is a dashboard labelled with key spelling concepts (i.e. suffixes, prefixes, silent letters), which helps them to introduce the focus for the unit.

The Spelling zone videos for Year 6/P7 revise key concepts taught in Years 2–5/P3–6.

Rapid recaps

In Session 2 of the units, the Spelling Team character from the video on Session 1 reappears and asks the children to quickly recap with their partner what they learnt in the previous session. This is to ensure that children are retaining the information.

Read Write Inc. Spelling resources

Extra Practice Zone

What is the Extra Practice Zone?

The Extra Practice Zone is part of the *Read Write Inc. Spelling* Online Resource with more than 1000 activity pages, providing further practice and consolidation for faster progress.

As shown in the screenshot below, the Extra Practice Zone can be accessed from the *Read Write Inc. Spelling* subscription homepage or from the hyperlinked Overview document.
A walkthrough video of the Extra Practice Zone is also available and is hyperlinked in the Overview document.

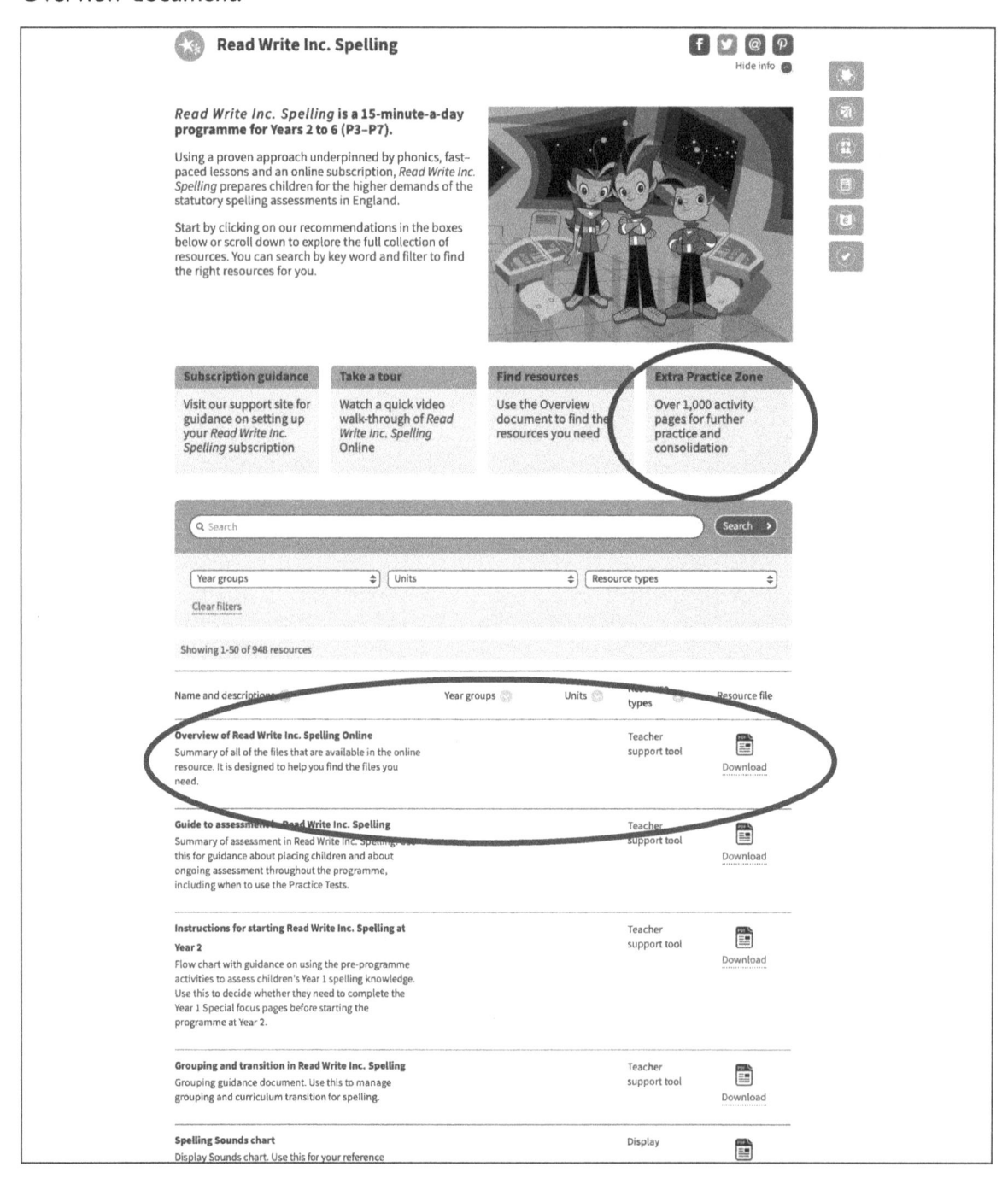

On the Extra Practice Zone, there are ten spelling areas from Y2/P3 to Y6/P7 (e.g. vowel graphemes, homophones, suffixes) and a variety of activity types (e.g. keying in, matching, multiple choice, highlighting).

The activities can be used in class via the *Read Write Inc. Spelling* Online Resource on Oxford Owl for School or accessed by pupils at home via My class login.

The activities provide easy and convenient revision practice for teachers, and fun practice for pupils with games included. They include common exception words from the National Curriculum, and provide children with a different form of practice, reviewing what they have been taught in the spelling programme.

How should I use the activities in the Extra Practice Zone?

The Extra Practice Zone activities can be used alongside the core spelling units, or for revision practice once all the units in one year group are completed.

The Extra Practice Zone Mapping Chart, which is available on the Online Resource, provides guidance on how the activities in the Extra Practice Zone can be incorporated into the Spelling programme. As shown in the screenshot below, the short-term revision tabs (separate tabs for Years 2–6/P3–7) break down the units in the Spelling programme, showing which activities are relevant to a particular unit. The long-term revision tab (one tab for all year groups) breaks down the activities in the Extra Practice Zone, showing which units are relevant to a particular activity.

Unit	Content	Rule/explanation	Examples	Extra Practice Zone Activities
Unit 1	The *or* sound spelt a before l and ll	In some words, the *or* sound is spelt a when it comes before l or ll. Remember that the letter l is silent.	all, tall, ball, call, fall, hall, wall etc. also, almost, always, already etc. talk, walk, chalk, stalk etc.	Spell the Vowel Odd Rhyme Out (Y3-6) Silent Letters (Y5-6)
Unit 2	Soft c	When c comes just before i, y or e, it usually makes the s sound. It is called **soft c**.	city, cell, exercise, icy, cycle, rice, mice, fancy, face, race etc.	
Special focus 1	Red words: where, could, there, want, was, would, what	**Red words** contain a sound with an **odd spelling** ... we need to *stop and think* about the odd part of the word before we write it.	See red words in column B	Odd Rhyme Out (Y3-6)
Unit 3	Adding the suffix -y (1) (to words ending in a short vowel and a consonant)	We can add -y to many root words to make adjectives. For some words, we **double** the final consonant before adding -y.	sloppy, funny, boggy, muddy, nutty, spotty etc.	Swap, Double or Drop? Spell the Root
Unit 4	Adding the suffix -y (2) (to words ending in e)	We can add -y to some root words ending in e to make adjectives. We **drop** the e before adding -y.	whiny, lazy, wavy, breezy, crazy, bony, smoky, shiny etc.	Swap, Double or Drop?
Special focus 2	Homophones: sea/see, son/sun, blew/blue, knight/night, saw/sore, quite/quiet	Words that sound the same but have different meanings and spellings are called **homophones**.	See homophones in column B	Sounds the Same
Unit 5	Adding the suffix -ly (to words to make adverbs)	We can add the suffix -ly to root words to make an adverb. When a word ends in a y, we **swap** the y for an i before adding -ly.	loudly, badly, bravely, stupidly etc. happily, easily etc.	Swap, Double or Drop? Rule Breakers Spell the Root
Unit 6	The *n* sound spelt kn and gn	Some words begin with the *n* sound spelt **kn**. It is a silent **k**. Silent k only ever comes before the letter n. The *n* sound at the start of words can also be spelt **gn**. This isn't a very common spelling! Like the silent k at the start of words, the silent g used to be said aloud.	knew, knot, knight, knit etc. gnat, gnaw, gnome, gnash etc.	Silent Letters (Y5-6)
Special focus 3	Red words: money, people, busy, half	**Red words** contain a sound with an **odd spelling** ... we need to *stop and think* about the odd part of the word before we write it.	See red words in column B	Odd Rhyme Out (Y3-6)
Unit 7	The *igh* sound spelt y	Lots of words end with the *igh* sound spelt y. If the end of a word sounds like *igh*, it is almost always spelt with a y.	shy, dry, fly, nearby, terrify etc.	Spell the Vowel
Unit 8	Adding the suffix -ing (1) (to words ending in a short vowel and a consonant)	If a word ends in a short vowel sound (*a, e, i, o, u*) + a consonant, we **double** the consonant before adding the suffix -ing. Never double the letters *w* or *x*.	putting, knotting, drumming, tripping, nodding, clapping etc.	Swap, Double or Drop? Rule Breakers Spell the Root
Special focus 4	Homophones: their/their, no/know, right/write, to/too.	Words that sound the same but have different meanings and spellings are called **homophones**.	See homophones in column B	Sounds the Same

short-term Y2A | short-term Y2B | short-term Y3 | short-term Y4 | short-term Y5 | short-term Y6 | long-term

What activities are included in the Extra Practice Zone?

Here are the ten types of activities:

- ☆ Spell the Vowel
- ☆ Sounds the Same
- ☆ Swap, Double or Drop
- ☆ Rule Breakers
- ☆ Playing with Plurals
- ☆ Word Endings
- ☆ Silent Letters
- ☆ Spell the Root
- ☆ Odd Sound Out
- ☆ Odd Rhyme Out

> See pp.62–63 for examples of these activities.
>
> Please see the Overview of the Extra Practice Zone for further details about each activity.
>
> Go to the main Overview document – the first one listed on the Online Resource – and scroll down to the Extra Practice Zone documents list.

How does the programme work?

Read Write Inc. Spelling teaches all of the spelling requirements of the National Curriculum in England. The requirements are divided into year groups, then subdivided into units of work. Each unit covers approximately one week of work, made up of five daily sessions of 15–20 minutes a day.

Route through *Read Write Inc. Spelling* for Year 2/P3

Children in Key Stage 1

Ensure children are ready to start the programme.
They should have finished or be about to finish their phonics programme so that they are reading fluently. For example, if your school is using *Read Write Inc. Phonics* children will be reading Grey Storybooks.

Complete pre-programme Year 1/P2 assessment and revision of phonics in *Practice Book 2A*.
If children need a reminder of any Year 1/P2 concepts, complete the optional activity pages to consolidate these on the Online Resource on Oxford Owl.

Complete Units 1–14 in *Practice Book 2A*
Complete Units 1–15 in *Practice Book 2B*

Complete **Special focus pages** in the order they appear in the Practice Book, or as a focused week at a time of your choosing.
Complete a **Consolidation session** (online) after every two units if children need extra practice.
Every half term, complete a **Practice test** (online). This prepares children for the assessment format.
Every unit, revisit the words in the online **Word banks** (in activities such as Speed spell, Team teach and Jumping Red/Orange words) to ensure children are confident with all the words they have learnt and may be assessed on.

End of Key Stage 1

You will have covered all of the statutory guidance for Year 2 of the National Curriculum in England (September 2014) and revisited key principles of Year 1 spelling that you have covered in your phonics teaching.

Route through *Read Write Inc. Spelling* for Years 3–6/P4–7

Start of Key Stage 2

Ensure children are ready to start the programme.
They should be fluent readers and have completed the spelling requirements up to and including Year 2 of the National Curriculum in England (Primary 3, Curriculum for Excellence for Scotland, Year 2 for Wales, and P3 for Northern Ireland).
If children need to revise key principles of phonics teaching, ask them to complete the **Pre-programme activities** online (see p.18).

⬇

Complete Units 1–14 in Year 3/P4
Complete Units 1–14 in Year 4/P5

Complete **Special focus pages** in the order they appear in the Practice Book, or as a focused week at a time of your choosing.
As for Year 2/P3, complete a **Consolidation session** (online) after every two units if children need extra practice.
Every half term, complete a **Practice test** (online). This prepares children for the assessment format.
Every unit, revisit the words in the online **Word banks** (in activities such as Speed spell, Team teach and Jumping Red/Orange words) to ensure children are confident with all the words they have learnt and may be assessed on.

⬇

Complete Units 1–12 in Year 5/P6

Note that Year 5 covers the content in the Year 5/6 section of the National Curriculum in England.
Complete **Special focus pages, Consolidation sessions** and **Practice tests** as specified above.

Complete Units 1–12 in Year 6/P7

Note that Year 6 revises key concepts taught in Years 2–5/P3–7.
Complete **Special focus pages, Consolidation sessions** and **Practice tests** as specified above.

⬇

End of Key Stage 2

You will have covered all of the statutory guidance for Years 3 and 4, and 5 and 6 of the National Curriculum in England.

See additional spelling sessions on p.17.

How does the programme work?

Timetables

The suggested weekly schedule follows the same basic pattern of activities for each unit. This means that as the children progress through the programme, you will spend less time explaining the activities and more time teaching children how to spell.

The plan opposite sets out a suggested order, but as you become familiar with the programme, there may be some activities that you skip through quickly and others that you wish to spend longer on, depending on the children's knowledge and memory. Remember, most activities will initially take a little longer while you and the children get into the swing of them.

It is important that you are flexible – the timings in the schedule are approximate. Some children may be able to work through each unit in a few sessions. It may be that some activities take longer and others less time, so an activity may need to continue in the following session.

Session	Activities
1	Speed spell
	Spelling zone
2	Rapid recap (online only)
	Dots and dashes
	Word changers
	Red and Orange words
3	Words to log and learn
	Dictation
	Red and Orange words
4	Four-in-a-row
	Choose the right word
	Red and Orange words
5	Team teach
	Jumping Red/Orange words

Flexible timetables

If you choose to organize children into spelling progress groups for spelling in your school, you will need to decide how many sessions children will spend on each unit and how much Spelling Log Book practice they need.

For example:

✶ Children with quick memories may only need four sessions per unit.

✶ Children who make steady progress may need five sessions per unit.

✶ Children who need a lot more practice may need seven sessions per unit.

How much time is needed?

We recommend spending 15–20 minutes for each session, daily, on the spelling activities.

The pace of progress will vary, depending on the ability and memory of the children. You may find that, in the higher years, children don't need to complete all the activities in each unit, although we do recommend full coverage in Years 2–4/Primary 3-5.

Alternatively, you may find that children benefit from using the Consolidation sessions to reinforce their learning, and that they require more time spent learning the Red/Orange words, in which case you will need to allow additional time to incorporate these activities.

Planning

Although there is flexibility as to how quickly you progress through *Read Write Inc. Spelling*, you may find these six-week example plans for each year group helpful.

Notes:

☆ Brackets indicate optional activities.

☆ Every week, Red and Orange words should be added to the Red/Orange word wall in the classroom, as children come across them in the programme.

☆ Every week, new words that children come across in their reading and use in their writing should be added to the Vocabulary Wall in the classroom.

Example plans for *Read Write Inc. Spelling*

Year 2/P3 (using *Practice Book 2A*)

Week 1	Week 2	Week 3	Week 4	Week 5	Week 6
Pre-programme activities (Pre-programme special focus pages)	Unit 1	Unit 2	Unit 3	Unit 4	Special focus 1, 2
					Practice test
					(Consolidation)
					(Spelling challenge)

Year 3/P4

Week 1	Week 2	Week 3	Week 4	Week 5	Week 6
Unit 1	Unit 2	Special focus 1	Unit 3	Unit 4	Practice test
		(Consolidation)			(Consolidation)
					(Spelling challenge)

Year 4/P5

Week 1	Week 2	Week 3	Week 4	Week 5	Week 6
Unit 1	Unit 2	Special focus 1	Unit 3	Unit 4	Practice test
		(Consolidation)			(Consolidation)
					(Spelling challenge)

Year 5/P6

Week 1	Week 2	Week 3	Week 4	Week 5	Week 6
Unit 1	Unit 2	Special focus 1, 2	Unit 3	Unit 4	Special focus 3, 4
		(Consolidation)			Practice test
					(Consolidation)
					(Spelling challenge)

Year 6/P7

Week 1	Week 2	Week 3	Week 4	Week 5	Week 6
Unit 1	Unit 2	Special focus 1, 2	Unit 3	Unit 4	Special focus 3, 4
		(Consolidation)			Practice test
					(Consolidation)
					(Spelling challenge)

Yearly timings for *Read Write Inc. Spelling*

These timings are based on an estimate of a unit taking five sessions to complete, assuming sessions are 15–20 minutes each day and children are working at an average pace.

Year 2/P3

Essential Year 2/P3 content	Number included	Estimated time to complete
Pre-programme activities	five activities	Up to a week
Units	14 in 2A, 15 in 2B	29 weeks
Special focus pages	seven in 2A, seven in 2B	14 sessions
Practice tests	six	six sessions
Estimated total time		**34 weeks**
Optional content: Consolidation sessions (online, 15); Year 1/P2 Practice tests (online, 2); Pre-programme special focus pages (online, 8)		up to 25 sessions

Year 3/P4

Essential Year 3/P4 content	Number included	Minimum time to complete
Units	14	14 weeks
Special focus pages	four	four sessions
Practice tests	six	six sessions
Estimated total time		**16 weeks**
Optional content: Consolidation sessions (online)	seven	seven sessions

Year 4/P5

Essential Year 4/P5 content	Number included	Minimum time to complete
Units	14	14 weeks
Special focus pages	four	four sessions
Practice tests	six	six sessions
Estimated total time		**16 weeks**
Optional content: Consolidation sessions (online)	seven	seven sessions

Year 5/P6

Essential Year 5/P6 content	Number included	Minimum time to complete
Units	12	12 weeks
Special focus pages	12	12 sessions
Practice tests	six	six sessions
Estimated total time		**16 weeks**
Optional content: Consolidation sessions (online)	six	six sessions

Year 6/P7

Essential Year 6/P7 content	Number included	Minimum time to complete
Units	12	12 weeks
Special focus pages	12	12 sessions
Practice tests	six (+ six challenge tests)	six sessions
Estimated total time		**16 weeks**
Optional content: Consolidation sessions (online)	six	six sessions

© Oxford University Press 2023. This page may be reproduced for use solely within the purchaser's school or college.

Yearly timings for *Read Write Inc. Spelling*

Additional spelling sessions

In addition to the core spelling units, there is a wide range of additional resources and activities available for further consolidation:

Special focus sessions

In addition to the five weekly sessions, the Practice Book units are interspersed with Special focus sessions, which look at particular topics or spellings that sometimes cause confusion. These Special focus topics include:

- short sessions for spelling concepts which do not require a complete unit
  e.g. the -il ending, which is uncommon
- Red words (words from the National Curriculum common exception word lists in Years 1 and 2, plus some high frequency words with unusual spellings)
- Orange words (words from the National Curriculum word lists in Years 3/4 and 5/6).
- homophones
- silent letters
- apostrophes
- contractions

Teaching support for the Special focus sessions can be found in the Online Resource, and the activities can be displayed in front of the whole class and discussed before children work on them individually in their Practice Books.

Although these Special focus sessions are interspersed between the main units in the Practice Books, they can be taught at any point in each yearly programme. In contrast, the main units are designed for teaching in the sequence suggested, to ensure that spelling knowledge is continually built upon and reinforced.

The Special focus sessions will take one or two daily spelling sessions. When planning, you will need to ensure that all the Special focus sessions are covered, as well as the main units. (See example plans on p.15.)

Consolidation sessions

Consolidation sessions (which are optional) are provided on the Online Resource after every two units. They are designed for further revision of what has been taught in the main units, and consist of two activities: Dictation and Choose the right word.

Practice tests

In the Online Resource, there are spelling tests for revision for each year group. These follow the same format as the end of Key Stage 1 and Key Stage 2 spelling tests, to familiarize children with the approach.

Dictionary and Thesaurus challenges

The Practice Books contain Dictionary challenges (Practice Books 3, 4, 5 and 6) and Thesaurus challenges (Practice Books 5 and 6). These activities extend children's vocabulary and give them practice in using a dictionary and thesaurus. They can be used with the whole class or for fast finishers.

Extra Practice Zone

The Extra Practice Zone activities on the Online Resource can be used alongside the core spelling units, or for revision practice once all the units in one year group are completed. See p.10 for further details about the Extra Practice Zone.

Pre-programme activities for assessment and revision of Year 1/P2 phonics and spelling

Before you start *Read Write Inc. Spelling*, work through the Pre-programme activities with the children. These are on pp.2–5 of *Practice Book 2A* and are also available on the Online Resource. The activities are designed to assess or revise children's understanding of the English alphabetic code, which is essential core knowledge on which they will build during the *Read Write Inc. Spelling* programme.

If children require further revision of the key spelling concepts covered in Year 1/P2 (other than phonics teaching), there is additional support for Year 1/P2 teaching online. The Pre-programme special focus pages online can be used to consolidate children's knowledge of key concepts from Year 1/P2.

Note that display/printable copies of all the Pre-programme activities can be found online. For activities that require written answers, there are completed activities online that can be displayed for whole-class demonstration. These should only be used after children have attempted the activities in their Practice Book first.

Key

Practice Book [PB]

Spelling Log Book [LB]

Online Resource on Oxford Owl for School

Materials printed from the Online Resource

Training films on the Ruth Miskin Training (RMT) online training subscription

Pre-programme Activity 1: Pure sounds

Purpose: to teach children how to pronounce the 44 speech sounds

Display Pre-programme Activity 1.

Tell the children that:

✭ We use 44 speech sounds to speak every word in the English language. These are divided into 24 *consonant* speech sounds and 20 *vowel* speech sounds.

(Note that the exact number of sounds is debated, but we have identified 44 key sounds for this programme. We have not included the *zh* sound in the chart because it is low frequency, nor schwa because it could be applied to many unstressed graphemes in the English language.)

✭ Consonant sounds are split into stretchy sounds and bouncy sounds. The stretchy sounds can be stretched as long as you can hold your breath; the bouncy sounds are short and cannot be stretched.

Consonant speech sounds

Use MTYT (My turn Your turn – see p.36) to show the children how to say the consonant speech sounds. Make sure they do not say *uh* at the end of each sound (*llll* not *luh*; *mmmm* not *muh*; *b* not *buh*; *c* not *cuh*). Note that the words (e.g. **b**oot, **c**at) show an example of that sound in a word.

Pre-programme activities for assessment and revision of Year 1/P2 phonics and spelling

Ask the children to take turns with a partner to listen to each other say the consonant sounds. The shaded boxes contain stretchy sounds.

b	c	ch	d	f	g	h	j	l	m	n	ng
as in boot	as in cat	as in chips	as in dog	as in fish	as in gate	as in hen	as in jam	as in leg	as in moon	as in net	as in king nk as in think*

p	qu	r	s	sh	t	th	v	w	x	y	z
as in pen	as in queen !	as in red	as in sun	as in shell	as in tree	as in thumb	as in vet	as in web	as in exercise !	as in yak	as in zebra

* nk = ng + k

The two boxes with ! in are really two speech sounds said at the same time. Please say them quickly and count them as one.

Vowel speech sounds

Use MTYT to show the children how to say the vowel speech sounds. Then ask them to practise with their partners. Note that the words (e.g. **a**t, h**e**n) show an example of that sound in a word.

a	e	i	o	u	ay	ee	igh	ow
as in at	as in hen	as in in	as in on	as in up	as in day	as in see	as in high	as in blow

oo	oo	ar	or	air	ir	ou	oy	ire	ear	ure
as in zoo	as in look	as in car	as in for	as in fair	as in whirl	as in shout	as in boy	as in fire	as in ear	as in pure

Pre-programme Activity 2: Same sound, different spelling

Purpose: to teach children that one sound is often spelt in more than one way

Display Pre-programme Activity 2.

Point out the charts in the activity. Explain that each box is a 'sound box' and that they will complete the boxes to show alternative spellings of each sound.

Point to the word lists in the boxes. Observe that each word has one grapheme written in bold, e.g. 'du**ck**'.

To demonstrate the grapheme in each word, use MTYT to:

☆ MTYT: 'ru**bb**le'

☆ TTYP: Which letters are in bold? Yes, double b.

☆ TTYP: Which sound does the double b make? Yes, 'b'.

☆ Write double b in the 'b' sound box.

Pre-programme activities for assessment and revision of Year 1/P2 phonics and spelling

Demonstrate for a few words before the children complete the activity.

After children have completed the activity in their Practice Books, display Pre-programme Activity 2: answers.

Pre-programme Activity 3: Dots and dashes

Purpose: for children to count the number of speech sounds in each word, including multi-syllabic words

Display Pre-programme Activity 3 (part 1).

Show the children how to:

- say words in speech sounds (use *bad, share* and *make* as examples)
- draw a dot for each speech sound written with a one-letter grapheme, e.g. bad
- draw a dash for each speech sound written with a two- or three-letter grapheme, e.g. share
- draw a 'smile' to indicate a split grapheme, e.g. make.

Ask the children to add dots, dashes and smiles to the words in their Practice Books.

Display Pre-programme Activity 3 (part 1): Answers.

Go through the words with the children, correcting any errors they have made.

Children can now move on to multi-syllabic words.

Display Pre-programme Activity 3 (part 2).

Tell the children that:

- the words in this box have more than one syllable
- when we say these words out loud, the syllables often get squashed together, so it is harder to know which speech sounds are in the word
- if we say these syllables very clearly and give them their 'full value', it makes spelling the words much easier. (The syllables in these words have been split in a way that makes it easy to say them out loud.)

Read the words and ask children to repeat them using MTYT. Repeat, saying each word in full value syllables.

Show the children how to:

- draw a dot for each speech sound written with a one-letter grapheme
- draw a dash for each speech sound written with a two- or three-letter grapheme
- draw a 'smile' to indicate a split grapheme, e.g. a-e.

Ask the children to add dots, dashes and smiles to the words in their Practice Books, then correct any errors with their partners.

Display Pre-programme Activity 3 (part 2): Answers.

Go through the words with the children, discussing any areas of uncertainty.

Pre-programme activities for assessment and revision of Year 1/P2 phonics and spelling

The *Read Write Inc. Spelling – Sounds Chart* will help you to check answers. Note that in some instances there is more than one way to dot and dash a word. For example, in the word **cage** we would usually suggest that the answer is cage: three sounds. However, the children will have learnt by Year 3/P4 that the *ay* sound can be spelt **a** and the *j* sound can be spelt **ge**, so they could also suggest cage.

There are some instances where we treat similar sounds differently to help children think carefully about them. In our answers we dash the ending **-le** as one sound (little) but dot each grapheme in **-el** (camel) and **-al** (tropical) to encourage children to think carefully about **-el** and **-al** endings, which often sound the same in everyday speech.

The important point for Dots and dashes is that the children carefully consider each sound, which helps them to remember how to spell the word.

Pre-programme Activity 4: Quiz 1

Purpose: to assess/revise children's knowledge of the alphabetic code

Display Pre-programme Activity 4.

To help children voice what they have learnt so far about the alphabetic code, ask them to answer these questions in their Practice Books with their partners:

1. How many speech sounds are there in the English language?
   - 44

2. What do we call a letter or group of letters that we use to write down one speech sound?
   - grapheme

3. Look at the charts you have just completed on p.3 of your Practice Book. How many different ways are there to spell each of these sounds: *f, m, r, s, ay, igh*?
   (Children should count the example grapheme in their answers. Note that children won't have written every possible spelling of each sound. You might like to point out some additional spellings, e.g. *ay* spelt **ei**, **aigh** or **ea**.)
   - *f*: three ways (f, ph, ff)
   - *m*: four ways (m, mb, mn, mm)
   - *r*: three ways (r, wr, rr)
   - *s*: five ways (s, c, ss, ce, se)
   - *ay*: four ways (ay, a-e, ai, eigh)
   - *igh*: five ways (igh, i-e, ie, y, i)

Display Pre-programme Activity 4: answers, or refer to the answers above.

After checking the answers with the whole class, see how quickly children can find sounds on the *Read Write Inc. Spelling – Sounds Chart* (display Pre-programme Activity 2: answers for this). Call out a few speech sounds from the charts, asking children to point to the correct sound box as quickly as they can.

Once the children can do this, ask them, in pairs, to take turns calling out a sound while their partner points to it on the chart. (They can use the charts on p.3 of *Practice Book 2A*.)

Pre-programme activities for assessment and revision of Year 1/P2 phonics and spelling

Pre-programme Activity 5: Quiz 2

Purpose: to assess children's knowledge of key concepts in the Year 1 National Curriculum

Display Pre-programme Activity 5.

Explain to the children that this is a quick quiz in their Practice Book. They should work on their own to complete it. Talk through the questions, ensuring they understand what they have to do, then ask children to complete the activities in their Practice Book.

When the children have completed the activities in their Practice Books, display Pre-programme Activity 5: Answers, and go through them as a class, noting any areas of confusion or uncertainty that need further revision.

If, after children have completed Activity 5, it becomes apparent that they need further consolidation of any of these concepts, there are printable one-page worksheets online. These relate to the questions in Activity 5 as follows:

Question	Concept assessed	Online support
1	Compound words	Pre-programme Special focus 1 Compound words
2	Syllables	Pre-programme Special focus 2 Syllables
3	Adding the prefix un- to a root word	Pre-programme Special focus 3 Adding the prefix un- to a root word
4	Adding -s and -es to words (plural of nouns and the third person singular of verbs)	Pre-programme Special focus 4 Adding -s to nouns and verbs to make plurals Pre-programme Special focus 5 Adding the endings -s and -es to nouns and verbs
5	Adding -er and -est to adjectives	Pre-programme Special focus 6 Adding -er and -est to adjectives
6	Adding the endings -ing, -ed and -er to verbs where no change is needed to the root word to verbs	Pre-programme Special focus 7 Adding the endings -ing and -ed to verbs Pre-programme Special focus 8 Adding -er to root words to make nouns

How a unit works

Children need:

☆ *Read Write Inc. Spelling* Practice Book

☆ *Read Write Inc. Spelling* Log Book

☆ A spelling jotter

☆ A sharp pencil (do not use pens)

☆ A junior dictionary in Years 3–6/P4–5 and a thesaurus in Years 5–6/P6–P7.

Teacher needs:

☆ *Read Write Inc. Spelling* – Sounds Chart

☆ An interactive whiteboard and pen

☆ A Red/Orange word wall (i.e. a space on a wall that you can develop into a Red/Orange word wall)

☆ A Vocabulary Wall for new and interesting words

☆ Words from the Word banks on the Online Resource, printed and cut up, plus your own record of words children are finding challenging.

Once the children have completed the pre-programme activities, they are ready to complete the same two key activities for each of the main units.

The sequence of activities in every unit follows the *Read Write Inc.* pedagogy, which is based on a continuous cycle of *learn something new, practice, consolidate in context, review*.

The activities below are divided into specified sessions, but you may wish to spend longer on some activities than others, depending on the needs of your children. The sequence of activities should remain the same in each unit, however long you spend on each activity.

Key

Practice Book [PB]

Spelling Log Book [LB]

Online Resource

Materials printed from the Online Resource

Training films on the Ruth Miskin Training (RMT) online training subscription

Session 1

Speed spell [PB] [LB]

Purpose: for children to review spellings from the previous unit

☆ Choose six of the words your children found most challenging from the previous unit to display. These can either be printed out from the Word bank or written on the board. (Note that for the first unit of *Practice Book 2A*, you will need to use words from the Word bank for Year 1/P2 on the Online Resource.)

23

How a unit works

✭ Use MTYT to say each word one by one. Hide the words and ask the children to write each word down in the space provided in their Practice Book.

Speed spell

Write the **Speed spell** words.

a _____ b _____ c _____

d _____ e _____ f _____

Circle any errors. Write the corrected spellings in your Log Book.

✭ Show the words and ask the children to check the spelling of the words they have written. Remind them to circle any incorrect graphemes and write the correct graphemes above. Then ask them to write the correct version of the word in their Spelling Log Book. Give feedback on the words that most children spelt correctly, and those that need more practice the following week.

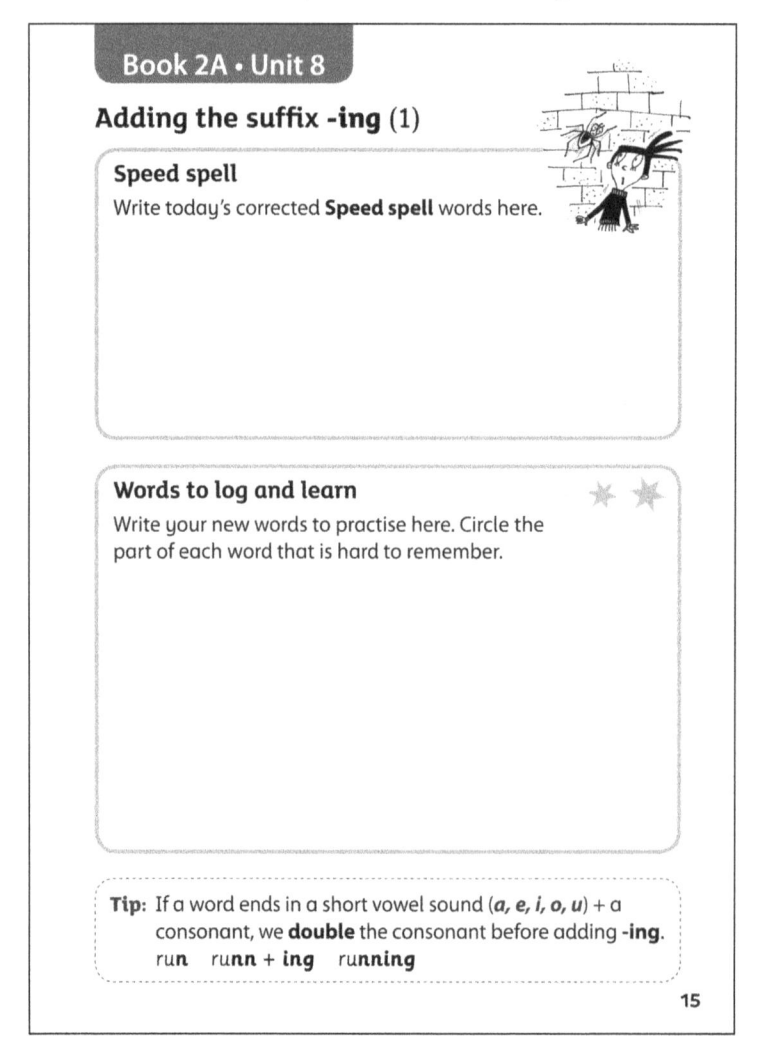

Book 2A • Unit 8

Adding the suffix -ing (1)

Speed spell
Write today's corrected **Speed spell** words here.

Words to log and learn
Write your new words to practise here. Circle the part of each word that is hard to remember.

Tip: If a word ends in a short vowel sound (*a, e, i, o, u*) + a consonant, we **double** the consonant before adding -**ing**.
run   runn + ing   running

15

How a unit works

Spelling zone 🅞 [PB]

Purpose: to introduce children to the focus of the unit

✲ Navigate to the correct unit on the Online Resource and play the Spelling zone video for the unit, in which the Spelling Star character introduces the focus for the unit. You may need to pause in places to allow time for partner talk or feedback. Ensure you pace the video to match the children's needs.

✲ The aliens will use the terms 'My turn Your turn' and 'Turn to your partner' in the videos (see pp.35–36). When the alien says 'Let's play My turn Your turn', ensure the children repeat the words after the alien has said them. When they ask children to 'Turn to your partner', ensure children turn to their partner to share an answer or repeat a key rule or rhyme. You may need to pause the videos to give the children more time to discuss.

running
stopping
batting
jogging

Introduction

A Star Speller character explains the focus of the unit.

✲ There are printable versions of the video scripts online for your reference.

✲ After watching the video, direct children to the Spelling zone activities in their Practice Books. There will be key information for children to read together and short activities to complete. If there is a rhyme to remember, a key rule or short phrase, ask children to TTYP (Turn to your partner) to repeat this and learn it by heart. Model one or two words before children complete the activity independently.

✲ Where children are asked to write sentences including key words, help them to write ambitious and meaningful sentences.

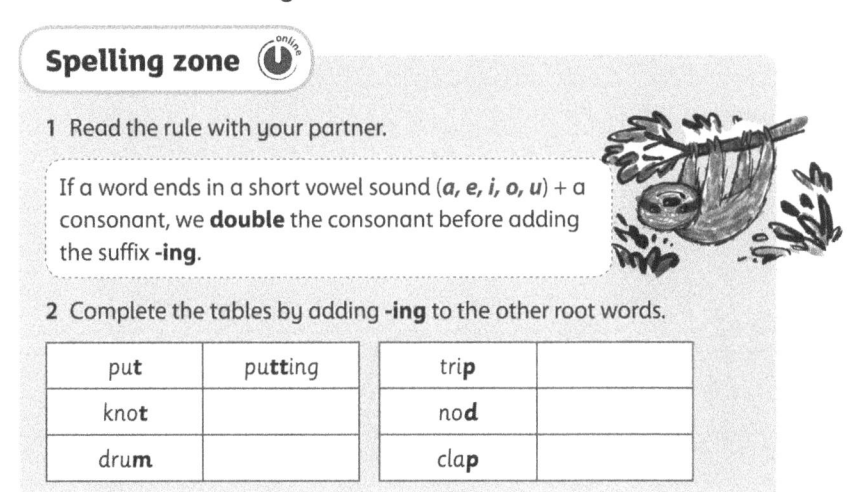

Spelling zone 🅞

1 Read the rule with your partner.

> If a word ends in a short vowel sound (*a, e, i, o, u*) + a consonant, we **double** the consonant before adding the suffix **-ing**.

2 Complete the tables by adding **-ing** to the other root words.

put	putting
knot	
drum	

tri**p**	
no**d**	
cla**p**	

✲ After each activity, display the words for children to check their spellings. Remind them to either tick, or circle the errors and write the correct grapheme above.

25

How a unit works

Dots and dashes PB (online)

Purpose: to help children to match speech sounds to graphemes

✫ Ask the children to open their Practice Books and complete the Dots and dashes table. Show the children how to complete the Dots and dashes table for two or three words:
- ask children to say the sounds
- write the total number of sounds for each word
- dot the graphemes written with one letter
- dash the graphemes written with two or three letters
- draw a 'smile' (link) to indicate a split grapheme, e.g. a-e, i-e, o-e, u-e
- circle the silent letters and not count them as a sound in the later years.

✫ If there are any Tips or Weird Word Warnings, discuss them with the children before they complete the activity. The Tips and Weird Word Warnings flag up points of interest about specific words and will help children to complete the activities correctly.

Dots and dashes (online)

Dot and dash the graphemes in the words. Write the number of sounds.

stop	4	slip		nod	
trot		flap		prod	
shop		grip		begin	
grab		chat		drop	
split		shrug		run	

✫ When children have completed their tables, display the Online Resource file with the answers for this activity for children to tick, or circle and correct their answers.

26

How a unit works

Session 2

Rapid recap

Purpose: to check that the children have retained the information that they learnt recently

✮ Navigate to the online file for this activity. The character who introduced the key focus in the previous session will ask the children to TTYP to recall the focus of the unit. Take feedback chorally or from two partners.

✮ If appropriate to the unit focus, ask all of the children to say the key rule, rhyme or phrase they learnt in the previous session's Spelling zone, chorally.

Word changers PB

Purpose: to help children to understand how a root word is affected by a suffix and/or prefix

✮ Remind the children what a root word is, i.e. the root gives the most meaning to a word and doesn't have a suffix or a prefix added.

✮ Tell the children that a prefix can be attached to the front of a root word and a suffix can be attached to the end of a root word.

✮ Explain that many new words can be built by adding prefixes and/or suffixes to root words.

✮ Where appropriate, explain how the word class can change, e.g. an adjective (kind) can become a noun (kindness).

✮ Show on the flipchart how to complete the word changers table for one or two words.

✮ Ask the children to complete the Word changers table in their Practice Book, after discussing any Tips or Weird Word Warnings.

Word changers

Complete the table.

root word	root word + suffix -ing
prod	prodding
begin	
spin	
nod	
shrug	
drop	
skip	
run	

27

How a unit works

* When they have completed their tables, display the Online Resource file for this activity. Follow the on-screen prompts to reveal the completed cells.

* Guide the children to tick and correct their own tables, checking with their partner if necessary.

Red and Orange words

In the Online Resource there are printable display copies of all the Red and Orange words in this programme.

Red words are common words that have an unusual spelling of a particular sound, e.g. said, the, would, my. They are called 'common exception words' in the National Curriculum for Years 1 and 2/P2 and 3.

Orange words are common words that are often misspelt by adults. These are taken from National Curriculum word lists for Years 3–6/P4–7, e.g. believe, straight, curiosity.

Red and Orange words are likely to be included in the spelling aspect of the Grammar, Punctuation and Spelling tests.

The Red and Orange words are taught in Sessions 1, 2, 3 and 4 each week (see Activities for teaching Red and Orange words on p.41). Children recall the spellings of Red and Orange words in the Jumping Red and Orange words activity.

Session 3

Words to log and learn [LB]

Purpose: for children to identify and record the words they need to practise

* Ask children to choose five words from Dots and dashes and Word changers that they have found challenging, then write them in their Spelling Log Book.

* Ask them to circle the part of the word they find hard to remember and to TTYP to explain why this is so.

Book 3 • Unit 6

Adding -ation to verbs to form nouns

Speed spell
Write today's corrected **Speed spell** words here.

Words to log and learn
Write your new words to practise here. Circle the part of each word that is hard to remember.

Tip: We can add the suffix **-ation** to verbs to make nouns.
  verb: inform   noun: inform**ation**
  If the verb ends with an **e** we **drop** the **e** before adding **-ation**.
  prepare + ation   prepar**ation**

Children write five words from the week's work that they particularly want to practise.

How a unit works

☆ Ask partners to take turns to discuss how they will remember to spell these words. (See pp.41–43 for suggested strategies for remembering tricky spellings.)

☆ Explain that these are the words that children should practise at home.

☆ Parents, carers or older siblings could be asked to review these words each week. The adult or older sibling calls out each word in turn and every time the child spells the word correctly, the adult or sibling writes their initials next to the word. (The child can either spell out the word aloud, or jot it down.)

Dictation PB (online)

Purpose: to help partners to practise the spellings in the context of a sentence

☆ Tell the children that they are now going to hear some of the words they have been spelling, in a full sentence.

☆ Explain that Partner 1:
- reads aloud for Partner 2 the first sentence from the relevant unit's dictation sentences at the back of their Practice Book
- watches carefully as Partner 2 writes the sentence in their Practice Book
- helps Partner 2 to check their sentence
- ticks each word, or circles and corrects the grapheme above.

Partner 1 dictation sentences

Unit 1
I am tall but you are taller.
We can walk while we talk.

Unit 8
The film is beginning now.
He was prodding it with a stick.

Unit 2
Three nice mice went into space.
The police officer won the race.

Unit 9
Alex is rattling the tin.
I am baking a huge cake.

☆ Partners swap roles after each sentence. There are two sentences for Partner 1 and two for Partner 2.

There are additional dictation sentences for extra practice in the Consolidation sessions online. There are also additional Challenge dictation sentences and More challenge dictation sentences on the Online Resource for fast finishers.

How a unit works

Session 4

Four-in-a-row PB

Purpose: to help children recall the spellings of words practised

✭ Show the children how to work with a partner to complete this activity. Partner 1:
  - chooses any word from Dots and dashes and Word changers which they think will challenge Partner 2
  - asks Partner 2 to write the word, without Partner 2 referring to the word in the Practice Book (in Year 2/P3, children can write the words in a jotter and in Years 3–6/P4–7, children can write the words in the lines given in their Practice Books)
  - ticks one of the shapes in Partner 2's Practice Book if the word is correct. If it isn't, Partner 1 helps Partner 2 to circle and correct.

✭ Partners swap roles after each word. The challenge is to see who can get four ticks first. If one child manages this, they are the winner. If both do this, they draw. You will need to ensure that each child has the same number of turns to make this activity fair.

> **Four-in-a-row**
>
> Choose a word from **Dots and dashes** or **Word changers** and say it to your partner. Ask them to write it down.
> Circle any wrong letters. If the word is right, tick a shape in your partner's book. Can you both spell four in a row correctly?

Choose the right word PB online

Purpose: to develop children's awareness of word families to reinforce spellings; to help children select the correct spelling so a sentence makes sense

✭ Explain that, like humans, words have relatives. In a word family, all the words are related to each other. Knowing how to spell one member of the word family can help you to spell its relations, e.g. joy, joyful, joyfully, joyfulness. (Note that in the National Curriculum in England glossary, a distinction is made between word inflections and word families, although in this programme we use the term 'word family' to cover both, in order to keep the concept accessible for children.)

How a unit works

☆ Note that for Year 2/P3, this is a class activity to be completed using the Online Resource. From Year 3/P4 onwards, the Online Resource can be used to demonstrate the activity before children complete it in their Practice Books. Then afterwards, it can be used to check answers as a class.

☆ Use 'drag and drop' on the Online Resource and your own TOL (Think out loud – i.e. saying your thought process aloud) to show the children how to select the correct word to complete a sentence, e.g. "I'm going to drag the word *concentrated* into this sentence. Let me read it out: 'The pupil is *concentrated* on her work.' Oh, that isn't right because *concentrated* is written in the past tense and the sentence is in the present tense, so I need to choose the word *concentrating*. Let me try that out ..." Show how you check all of the options.

☆ Now work through the rest of the activity. You may wish to ask children to vote in partners or teams as to which word they think is correct.

Choose the right word

Complete the sentences using the correct word from each word family.

> visible   invisible   disapprove   approved   approve
> unsafe   safe   complete   incomplete

1 The boy had the power to make himself _____ .
2 After the rain, a rainbow was _____ in the sky.
3 Dad will _____ of my messy bedroom.
4 I think my teacher will _____ of my neat handwriting.

Session 5
Team teach

Purpose: for children to work as a group to review and revise words from the current unit and words from their Spelling Log Books

☆ Join sets of partners together to make teams of four or six.

☆ Using the activities completed so far as a guide, choose ten words from the Word bank (available on the Online Resource) or your own records. These should be words you think the children have found the most challenging. Print and cut up or make enough for one set of words per team.

31

How a unit works

because	behind
both	bought
break	brother

- ✧ Model how you order the words into levels of difficulty by identifying the challenging part of each particular word. Then ask the children to work together to order their words. Explain that they must come to an agreement on the order.

- ✧ Now ask them to elect a team leader who will stack the words with the easiest on top.

- ✧ Explain that the team leader will call out the top word for others in the group to spell.

- ✧ After it has been spelt, the team leader must then turn the card around for the children to check and correct their spelling.

- ✧ Ask them to repeat the process until you tell them to stop.

- ✧ Explain that they should order the words into levels of difficulty again, making changes where relevant according to which words they found challenging.

Jumping Red/Orange words

Purpose: to help children recall the spellings of Red and Orange words

- ✧ Decorate an empty shoe box and label it as a 'Jumping word box'.

- ✧ Keep your own spelling log of Red/Orange words that children are misspelling. (You could include additional words if children are misspelling them frequently.)

- ✧ Write these words on strips of paper or card, or print them out from the online Word bank. Place these 'jumping words' in the box. Each week, choose six of these words to teach.

- ✧ In this activity, children spell the Red and/or Orange words they have practised that week. Read out the six words and ask children to write them in their Practice Book.

- ✧ Display the words and ask children to tick, or circle and correct. Tell them that the words can only 'jump' out of the box when you feel everyone can spell them confidently. They must go back in again if they are misspelt in future written work (so do keep hold of them).

- ✧ In their Spelling Log Books, children can note down Red/Orange words that they want to practise and ones that they already know.

Word walls

In the classroom, create wall space on which to display words that you meet as you progress through the activities. Display:

- Red and Orange words
- exciting words that will extend children's vocabulary.

If you are using *Read Write Inc. Phonics* or *Read Write Inc. Literacy and Language*, you will already have a pocket chart or wall devoted to new vocabulary. Ensure that children understand the meaning of all the words on display, as well as being able to spell them.

Remove words from your Red/Orange word wall when you feel the children are confident spelling them, in order to make room for a new word – there are more than 250 in total! You could perform a 'ceremony' when a Red/Orange word is taken off the wall.

Team teach: spelling challenge

At the end of each half term you may wish to organize a Spelling challenge by collecting 50–100 words from the children's Spelling Log Books and your own log. (These will vary according to the class.) The Spelling challenge is an extended Team teach activity. It lasts for up to a week and encourages children to work together as a group to help all members of the group improve their spelling.

Put children into groups of four to six mixed spellers. Ask the groups to practise spelling the 50–100 words you have chosen, in preparation for the group Spelling challenge on the final day of the week. See the Team teach instructions on p.31 for guidance on how children should work together to help each other to learn the words. You could ask children to prepare their own word cards, to give them further practice writing the words. Alternatively, print words from the online Word bank or use the cards you have prepared previously for Team teach.

Guide the children to focus on the words they find most challenging (i.e. the ten words at the bottom of the stack) and to rearrange the stack each day. Support children who need the most help. Encourage children to practise at home.

On the Spelling challenge day, you are the caller. Select at least 30 words (from your initial selection of 50–100) to test. Ask children to write the words individually as you call them. After the test, ask the children to check and correct their words as you display the correct spellings one by one.

Total the joint scores of all the children in each group and ask the winning group to nominate a treat that benefits everyone.

Classroom management

How should the children be grouped?

There are three options for how to group the children:

- ✩ Option one: Teach a whole class together.
- ✩ Option two: Organize children into spelling progress groups across two year groups or one year group in a large school.
- ✩ Option three: Split a class into two progress groups. Teach the teacher-led activities to one group while the other group complete the practice activities. Swap each day.

This programme is designed primarily for whole-class teaching, rather than group work. Some children may require catch-up lessons in order to reach the required standard before they can participate in these whole-class sessions. Use the Pre-programme activities on pp. 18–22 to assess or refresh children's understanding.

Where do children sit during the lesson?

Children sit at their tables, side-by-side with a partner, with easy view of you and the board, as well as the Red/Orange word wall and the Vocabulary Wall. Note that the latter two may need to be hidden when you are testing the children's spellings, or if they are testing each other or themselves.

The five principles

We have five core principles to teaching and learning. These are to:

1. know the PURPOSE of every activity and share it with the children, so children know the one thing they should be thinking about;
2. be PASSIONATE about teaching so you can engage children emotionally;
3. teach at an effective PACE and devote every moment to teaching and learning;
4. ensure that every child PARTICIPATES throughout the lesson. Partner work is fundamental to learning;
5. PRAISE effort and progress – not ability.

1. Purpose

We can only pay attention to one new thing at a time. If we are asked to learn too much at once, we give up. Each activity in the programme has one very clear purpose. It is important to set the purpose at the beginning of each activity so the children understand what they are learning and why.

2. Passion

Emotional engagement is necessary for children to learn something new. The greater their engagement, the more they learn. Children mirror your mood. When you are enthusiastic, children are too.

Show your passion for teaching:

✲ Smile. If you aren't enjoying the lesson, the children won't either.

✲ Love the children who need winning over – they need you more than all the others. When you enjoy having them in your lesson, they misbehave less.

✲ Prepare thoroughly so you can concentrate on children's progress.

3. Pace

Signals to keep the pace
We need children's minds to be free to learn to read and write. This means practising routines until they become second nature.

Silent signals
Praise children for routines they do quickly and quietly. However, once children know the routines, acknowledge their co-operation with a nod, a smile or a thank you.

Team stop signal
The team stop signal helps us stop children in a calm manner, ready for what's next. Use this signal to gain attention. Practise until children respond in under five seconds and in silence. It replaces all other stopping techniques: clapping, clicking, singing rhymes, shaking maracas, shouting, shushing, dance routines, counting back.

Use the stop signal at playtime, in assembly, in lessons, during transitions, at lunchtime, on trips and in staff meetings.

Turn to your partner (TTYP) signal
Partner work should be used consistently in all lessons. This signal indicates children should turn to their partners to answer the question. See 'Participation' on p.36.

Classroom management

My turn Your turn (MTYT) signal
Use this silent signal when you want the children to repeat something after you.

1, 2, 3 signal
Use this silent signal to move the children silently from tables to carpet in under 15 seconds.

Silent handwriting signal
Use this silent signal to indicate children should sit in the correct handwriting position.

4. Participation

Teamwork
We want children to be motivated to work together, teach each other, practise together, talk together, give feedback to each other. Teamwork is key.

Partnerships
Partner work is an important feature of this programme. Children should work with a partner who is at about the same level of spelling ability; they can have more fun learning and can help each other as well. When children discuss the words they are learning to spell, it is more likely they will remember them.

If you are teaching an individual child away from the class, you may choose to be the second partner.

In all circumstances, the teacher decides on the partnerships. They should be chosen with care and rotated every few weeks.

It is important to consider how well different children will work together.

Try to avoid odd numbers, but if this is unavoidable, put three well-motivated children together.

Classroom management

Remember, if a question is worth asking, it's worth everyone answering. All children should answer all questions by discussing them with their partners (except when children are working together in a group). Whatever the question, children should never raise their hands. If this is allowed, you will give the message that only a few need to answer.

In order to establish good partner work, it is important to examine, with the children, what is involved in working with a partner (e.g. remind them to praise their partner and to be polite to each other at all times).

1. Articulating a thought forces children to engage. It makes them organize what they know and what they don't know. This is why we want all children to practise what they have been taught with a partner throughout every lesson. They practise every activity and answer every question together. Organize new partnerships every four to six weeks.

2. Children need to pay attention to their partners. They only do this if they feel comfortable working with them. Use a Partner Quiz to help new partners build a relationship: ask partners to find out their partner's favourite food/TV programme/film/computer game/story and what makes them cross, happy, and so on.

3. Praise effective partner work throughout the day, until it becomes 'what you do'.

4. Some partnerships are more successful than others, but stick with it – if you take partnerships seriously, the children will, too.

No hands-up, thumbs-up, chests-up!
We strongly discourage hands-up or thumbs-up (or chests-up!) as a technique for answering questions. In 'hands-up' classrooms, few children respond to questions. Children who don't raise their hands are unlikely to pay attention.

We also discourage the 'pull out the stick' technique. Again, any one question is only answered by a few children.

We gain and keep children's attention throughout the lesson by using three techniques: choral work, partner practice and partner talk.

Choral work: My turn Your turn (MTYT)
We use choral work when we want children to copy what we've just said.

Partner talk
Children pay attention because they know they will be expected to answer every question with their partner and could be called upon to share their response with the rest of the group.

Routines for partner talk
1. Ask the question.

2. Use the TTYP silent signal.

3. Listen as children prepare an answer with their partner.

4. Use the stop signal.

5. Select feedback methods.

Explain that you expect both partners to prepare an answer and that you will choose how feedback is collected, i.e. you will no longer choose children to answer questions who raise their hands or thumbs. Observe partners as they talk – don't get stuck with one partner.

Classroom management

Feedback methods

Use Choose Two for responses requiring explanations and reasons. Select two partners who have answers you can build upon. (Choose children who have not raised their hands/thumbs to answer.)

Use Choral Response when there is only one correct answer. Ask children to respond together by gesturing towards them with both hands (Your turn signal).

Paraphrase some of the children's responses that you heard during TTYP to keep the discussion moving or when you want to feed back on behalf of a child who isn't yet confident to talk to the whole group.

Use Word Wave for one-word answers with multiple responses. Ask children to call out their answers as you move your hand across the group.

5. Positive teaching

It is really worth winning over children who might potentially be uncooperative. Check these children are near you in your direct line of vision. Give them responsibility. For example, ask the child to help you model correct partner behaviour or to start the stop signal – and praise them for working well as a team.

Praise effort

There is no field of learning where a huge amount of practice is not essential: sport, music, dancing, science, mathematics – and learning to spell is no exception.

Children must understand that effort is always required to learn something new – that sometimes things are hard to learn and therefore they need to practise even harder. Children feel good when they are working hard and succeeding.

So praise effort and be specific, for example:

- "Well done, I can see that you've worked very hard on learning those words."
- "You're putting in a lot of effort into remembering the spelling rules here."
- "You've really improved your spelling of challenging words this week."

Praise the child quietly. For every child you praise loudly, there are another three children who are disappointed you didn't praise them.

Be genuine – only praise when there is a good reason. Children know when they deserve your praise.

Praise partner work

Praise children for the way partners work together. For example:

"Great team work:

- You **both** listened carefully to each other."
- You **both** have an answer."
- You **both** worked so hard."

Praise that doesn't work
Don't praise children's ability
If you praise children for being clever at something, you draw attention to 'ability' as something that is in short supply, i.e. only some children have it.

The not-praised-for-being-clever-children think: 'I'm not clever. I can't do this. It's not worth trying.'

The praised-for-being-clever-children think: 'I am clever. I find it easy.' However, when things get hard they think: 'Uh-oh. This is difficult. If I were really clever I wouldn't have to try hard. Maybe I am not clever.'

Behaviour that stops children learning
If you do this then you will get rewards: stickers, tokens and points
Stickers, tokens and points do not help children learn in the long term. By rewarding an activity that should be intrinsically rewarding, we send the message to children that the activity, i.e. spelling, is not pleasant and that nobody would do it without a bribe. We must avoid, at all cost, building a culture of payment for learning.

Children who receive stickers think: 'I get stickers for spelling. No one else gets them. I can't be clever.' Or 'I like stickers. I will work hard for the next sticker but if I don't get a sticker I won't work hard.'

Anger
Anger and anxiety disable children's ability to learn and work hard. It puts them into the debilitating mode of freeze, flight or fright. Teachers who use punishments, sanctions, criticism, shouting, sarcasm, belittlement, rudeness and frowning may achieve compliance from children but destroy any willingness to learn. Use positive teaching methods combined with the other principles to ensure that you do not have to resort to anger in lessons.

Terminology and progression

We generally use grammatical terminology such as *noun*, *verb* and *adjective*. The terms are introduced and explained in the online videos where necessary, and there is a brief definition for children's reference in the Log Book glossaries (inside the front cover of each Log Book).

Please note that some example words (which are suggested in the National Curriculum) may be challenging for some children. We have suggested guidance for how you can clarify these. Naturally, you may need to clarify some other words with your class, depending on the needs of your children.

There are some places in Year 2/P3 where we do not explain the full detail of a spelling rule or include all of the non-statutory guidance in one unit because we feel it would be unmanageable for some Year 2/P3 children. In these instances, the rules are expanded and consolidated later in the Year 2/P3 teaching or later in the programme.

In some places we have been flexible with terminology, for ease of teaching. For example:

Word families Grammarians argue over the exact definition of 'word family' and how words might be divided into 'word family words' and inflections of the verb. To keep the concept accessible for younger children, we sometimes include verb inflections in lists of word family words.

Root words We generally define root words as the part of the word that gives the most meaning, which does not have any suffixes or prefixes added. However, we are occasionally flexible with this definition where the strict root form of a word is not commonly used (i.e. we call 'politics' a root word rather than 'politic' as we feel it is easier for children to understand).

How do we ensure all children make progress?

- Children are introduced to spelling rules and patterns from the start of the programme. These are reviewed and practised through each unit until all children can apply the rules in their own writing.
- Group and team activities can be tailored to the needs of the children. In activities such as Team teach, the teacher can select words for each group that they think children particularly need to practise.
- In several activities (Words to log and learn, Four-in-a-row, Jumping Red/Orange words) children focus on the words they personally need to practise so the teacher can encourage them to choose words appropriate to their learning needs.
- The Year 6/P7 Practice tests include six Challenge tests, designed to stretch higher ability children. For children who need more support at the start of the programme, two Year 1/P2 Practice tests are provided for consolidation and assessment.
- Consolidation sessions (online) can be used with the whole class or with smaller groups to give extra support.
- Challenge dictation sentences and More challenge dictation sentences are available online for fast finishers. In Practice Books 3–6 there are Dictionary challenges which can be completed by fast finishers. In Practice Books 5 and 6 there are also Thesaurus challenges.

Terminology and progression

Activities for teaching Red and Orange words

Red and Orange words are taught in Sessions 2, 3 and 4. Each week, choose six Red or Orange words to teach. Display the words in your pocket chart. There are five activities to teach children to spell Red or Orange words: Mnemonics, Say it as it looks, Word in a word, A sticky letter, Rap it.

Mnemonics

A mnemonic connects something that is hard to remember with a memorable phrase. Use mnemonic phrases to help children learn the trickiest words. Here are some suggested mnemonics or you can have fun helping children decide their own:

- w**ould**, c**ould**, sh**ould**, sh**ould**er: *oh you (u) lovely darling*
- r**ough**, en**ough**, th**ough**, th**ough**t, b**ough**t: *oh you (u) great hooligan*
- c**augh**t, d**augh**ter, n**augh**ty, l**augh**: *ants usually get hot*
- s**ai**d: *it's got an 'a' and an 'i', but I don't know why*
- **because**: *big elephants can't always use small entrances.* Draw an illustration and label this phrase.

Use the following method to explain the mnemonics, e.g. 'would, could, should, shoulder' (tricky bit: ould):

- Write the word on the board.
- MTYT: "would".
- Say "W oh you lovely darling" as you point to each letter.
- Ask children to say the mnemonic MTYT and then to their partner.
- Repeat this method with the other words.
- Then rub all the words off the board.
- Ask children to write each word as they say the spelling out loud, in whispers, then silently.
- Ask children to tick the word if it is correct. If it is wrong, circle the errors and write the correct grapheme above.

NB: Don't use too many mnemonics. Sometimes it is easier to remember the word than the mnemonic.

Say it as it looks

We teach children to 'say it as it looks' to help them remember the correct spelling. Here are some examples:

- wh**a**t, w**a**tch, w**a**s (say *a* as in **a**pple)
- pr**e**tty (say *e* as in **e**gg)
- tw**o** (say twoh)
- d**oe**s, d**oe**sn't (say *oe* as in t**oe**)
- m**o**ther, an**o**ther, br**o**ther (say *o* as in h**o**t).

Terminology and progression

Use the following method to say it as it looks, e.g. 'what, watch, was':

☆ Write the word on the board.

☆ Say the word as it looks. MTYT, TTYP. "what" (say *a* as in **a**pple).

☆ Say the word within a sentence: "What (as in **a**pple) do you think you're doing?"

☆ Repeat this method with the other words.

☆ Then rub all the words off the board.

☆ Ask the children to write each word as they say it out loud.

☆ Ask children to tick, or circle and correct.

Word in a word

Sometimes we can help children to remember a spelling by noticing that there is a 'word in a word'. Here are some examples:

☆ **bus**y on the **bus**

☆ **one** thing I have **gone** and d**one**

☆ **bus**iness on the **bus**

☆ **or** in w**or**k, w**or**d, w**or**se

☆ **ear** in l**ear**n, **ear**th, h**ear**t

☆ **our** in y**our** and f**our**

☆ **me** in co**me** and so**me**

☆ **all** in sm**all**, b**all**, t**all**

☆ **any** in m**any**.

Use the following method to draw attention to words within words, e.g. 'busy on the bus':

☆ Write the words on the board.

☆ Say "it's busy on the bus" (say "bussy", not "bizzy").

☆ Ask children to TTYP to find a word in the word.

☆ Take feedback.

☆ Then rub all the words off the board.

☆ Ask the children to write each word as they say the spelling out loud, in whispers, then silently.

☆ Ask children to tick, circle or correct each word.

A sticky letter

Some words are often spelt incorrectly because of one tricky or 'sticky' letter. Sticky letters help when there is only one letter causing a problem.

Write the word and then draw something in the shape of the letter.

Terminology and progression

- **o** in pe**o**ple: draw a face
- **i** in fr**i**end: draw your friend – dot for the head, stick for the body
- **i** in ju**i**cy: draw a lolly or fruit
- **u** in b**u**ild: draw a house
- **l** in wa**l**k and ta**l**k: draw a leg
- **u** in bisc**u**it: draw half a biscuit
- **o** in y**o**ung: draw a baby in its cot
- **w** in **w**ho: draw a worm.

Use the following method to show sticky letters, e.g. 'people':

- Write the word on the board.
- Say the word using MTYT: "people".
- TTYP: Where is the sticky letter? (o)
- Draw a picture of a face inside the o.
- Repeat this method with the other words.
- Then rub all the words off the board.
- Ask the children to write each word as they say the spelling out loud, in whispers, then silently.
- Ask children to tick, or circle and correct each word.

Rap it

In Rap it, we say the letter names in a rhythm to help children to remember the word.

Say the word, then the graphemes in a rhythm and then repeat the word again.

- Where ... wh-ere ... where
- There ... th-ere ... there
- Were ... w-ere ... were.

Use the following method to 'rap it', e.g. 'where':

- Write the word on the board.
- Say the word using MTYT: "where".
- Say the spelling in letter names, running together the letter names that make a grapheme: "WH-ERE" *doubleuaitch-eearee*.
- Develop a rap rhythm as you say the letter names: "WH-ERE".
- Repeat this method with the other words.
- Then rub all the words off the board.
- Ask the children to write each word as they say the rhythm out loud, in whispers, then silently.
- Ask children to tick, or circle and correct.

Read Write Inc. Spelling content matched to National Curriculum English Appendix 1: Spelling

These grids show the unit order in the *Read Write Inc. Spelling* programme. There are additional grids in the Online Resource which follow the National Curriculum in England order, with the correlating units alongside.

Practice Book 2A, Log Book 2, Online 2

Section	Content	Link to National Curriculum requirements (English Appendix 1: Spelling)
Pre-programme activities	Revision of the English alphabetic code and of key concepts from Year 1	Year 1 spelling curriculum content
Unit 1	The *or* sound spelt **a** before **l** and **ll**	The /ɔː/ sound spelt a before l and ll
Unit 2	Soft **c**	The /s/ sound spelt c before e, i and y
Special focus 1	Red words: *where, could, there, want, was, would, what*	Years 1 and 2 common exception words
Unit 3	Adding the suffix **-y** (1) (to words ending in a short vowel and a consonant)	Adding -ing, -ed, -er, -est and -y to words of one syllable ending in a single consonant letter after a single vowel letter
Unit 4	Adding the suffix **-y** (2) (to words ending in **e**)	Adding the endings -ing, -ed, -er, -est and -y to words ending in -e with a consonant before it
Special focus 2	Homophones: *sea/sea, son/sun, blew/blue, knight/night, saw/sore, quite/quiet*	Year 2 homophones and near-homophones
Unit 5	Adding the suffix **-ly** (to words to make adverbs)	The suffixes -ment, -ness, -ful, -less and -ly
Unit 6	The *n* sound spelt **kn** and **gn**	The /n/ sound spelt kn and (less often) gn at the beginning of words
Special focus 3	Red words: *money, people, busy, half*	Year 2 common exception words
Unit 7	The *igh* sound spelt **y**	The /aɪ/ sound spelt -y at the end of words
Unit 8	Adding the suffix **-ing** (1) (to words ending in a short vowel and a consonant)	Adding -ing, -ed, -er, -est and -y to words of one syllable ending in a single consonant letter after a single vowel letter
Special focus 4	Homophones: *there/their, no/know, right/write, to/too, week/weak, see/sea*	Year 2 homophones
Unit 9	Adding the suffix **-ing** (2) (to words ending in **e** or **ie**)	Adding the endings -ing, -ed, -er, -est and -y to words ending in -e with a consonant before it
Unit 10	The *j* sound	The /dʒ/ sound spelt as ge and dge at the end of words, and sometimes spelt as g elsewhere in words before e, i and y

44

© Oxford University Press 2023. This page may be reproduced for use solely within the purchaser's school or college.

Read Write Inc. Spelling content matched to the National Curriculum

Section	Content	Link to National Curriculum requirements (English Appendix 1: Spelling)
Special focus 5	Contractions and apostrophes: *I'm, I'll, you're, he's, they're, she'll, we're*	Contractions The possessive apostrophe (singular nouns)
Unit 11	The **o** sound spelt **a** after **w** and **qu**	The /ɒ/ sound spelt a after w and qu
Unit 12	Adding the suffix **-ed** (1) (to words ending in two consonant letters and words ending in a short vowel and a consonant)	Adding -ing, -ed, -er, -est and -y to words of one syllable ending in a single consonant letter after a single vowel letter
Special focus 6	The **u** sound spelt **o**, and the **or** sound spelt **ar** after **w**: *mother, brother, other, nothing, Monday, towards, swarm, reward, warm*	The /ʌ/ sound spelt o The /ɔː/ sound spelt ar after w
Unit 13	Adding the suffix **-ed** (2) (swapping **y** for **i**)	Adding -ed, -ing, -er and -est to a root word ending in -y with a consonant before it
Unit 14	Adding the suffix **-ed** (3) (dropping **e** to add **-ed**, and revision of doubling the final consonant and swapping **y** for **i**)	Adding the endings -ing, -ed, -er, -est and -y to words ending in -e with a consonant before it
Special focus 7	Possessive apostrophes	The possessive apostrophe (singular nouns)

45

© Oxford University Press 2023. This page may be reproduced for use solely within the purchaser's school or college.

Read Write Inc. Spelling content matched to the National Curriculum

Practice Book 2B, Log Book 2, Online 2

Section	Content	Link to National Curriculum requirements (English Appendix 1: Spelling)
Unit 1	The *r* sound spelt **wr**	The /r/ sound spelt wr at the beginning of words
Unit 2	Adding the suffixes **-er** or **-est** (1) (words where no change is needed; words ending in **e**)	Adding the endings -ing, -ed, -er, -est and -y to words ending in -e with a consonant before it
Special focus 1	Red words: *many, some, should, come, any, would*	Years 1 and 2 common exception words
Unit 3	Adding the suffixes **-er** or **-est** (2) (swapping **y** for **i**)	Adding -ed, -ing, -er and -est to a root word ending in -y with a consonant before it
Unit 4	Adding the suffixes **-er** or **-est** (3) (doubling consonant, where the root word ends in short vowel plus consonant)	Adding -ing, -ed, -er, -est and -y to words of one syllable ending in a single consonant letter after a single vowel letter
Special focus 2	Homophones: *see/sea, there/their, too/two, for/four, nose/knows, ate/eight*	Year 2 homophones
Unit 5	The **ee** sound spelt **ey**	The /iː/ sound spelt -ey
Unit 6	Adding the suffix **-ness** (1) (adding to a root word where no change is needed to the root word)	The suffixes -ment, -ness, -ful, -less and -ly
Special focus 3	Words ending in **-il** and words where **s** makes the **zh** sound: *pupil, pencil, fossil, nostril, evil, stencil, council, peril, treasure, usual, television, revision, measure*	Words ending -il The /ʒ/ sound spelt s
Unit 7	Adding the suffix **-ness** (2) (swapping **y** for **i**)	The suffixes -ment, -ness, -ful, -less and -ly
Unit 8	Words ending in **-le**	The /l/ or /əl/ sound spelt -le at the end of words
Special focus 4	Homophones: *seen/scene, wait/weight, hole/whole, sighed/side, new/knew*	Years 3 and 4 homophones
Unit 9	Words ending in **-el**	The /l/ or /əl/ sound spelt -el at the end of words
Unit 10	Words ending in **-al**	The /l/ or /əl/ sound spelt -al at the end of words
Special focus 5	The *ir* sound spelt **or** after **w**: *worm, world, work, worth, worst, worse, password, workshop, workers*	The /ɜː/ sound spelt or after w
Unit 11	Adding the suffix **-ful**	The suffixes -ment, -ness, -ful, -less and -ly
Unit 12	Adding the suffix **-less**	The suffixes -ment, -ness, -ful, -less and -ly
Special focus 6	Contractions and apostrophes: *I've, we'd, they've, you've, you'd, they'd*	Contractions
Unit 13	Adding the suffix **-ment**	The suffixes -ment, -ness, -ful, -less and -ly
Unit 14	Words ending in **-tion**	Words ending in -tion
Unit 15	Adding the suffix **-es**	Adding -es to nouns and verbs ending in -y
Special focus 7	Possessive apostrophes	The possessive apostrophe (singular nouns)

© Oxford University Press 2023. This page may be reproduced for use solely within the purchaser's school or college.

Read Write Inc. Spelling content matched to the National Curriculum

Practice Book 3, Log Books 3–4, Online 3

Section	Content	Link to National Curriculum requirements (English Appendix 1: Spelling)
Unit 1	Adding the prefixes **dis-** and **in-**	More prefixes
Unit 2	Adding **im-** to root words beginning with **m** or **p**	More prefixes
Special focus 1	Orange words: *answer, island, February, length, strength, business*	Years 3 and 4 word list
Unit 3	Adding the suffix **-ous**	The suffix -ous
Unit 4	Adding the suffix **-ly** (to adjectives to form adverbs)	The suffix -ly
Unit 5	Words ending in **-ture**	Words with endings sounding like /ʒə/ or /tʃə/
Special focus 2	Homophones: *no/know, write/right, where/wear, meet/meat, great/grate, bear/bare, break/brake, week/weak*	Years 3 and 4 homophones
Unit 6	Adding **-ation** to verbs to form nouns	The suffix -ation
Unit 7	Words with the **c** sound spelt **ch**	Words with the /k/ sound spelt ch (Greek in origin)
Unit 8	Words with the **sh** sound spelt **ch**	Words with the /ʃ/ sound spelt ch (mostly French in origin)
Special focus 3	The short *i* sound spelt **y**: *myth, Egypt, gym, pyramid, mysterious*	The /ɪ/ sound spelt y elsewhere than at the end of words
Unit 9	Adding the suffix **-ion** (to root words ending in **t** or **te**)	Endings which sound like /ʃən/, spelt -tion, -sion, -ssion, -cian
Unit 10	Adding the suffix **-ian** (to root words ending in **c** or **cs**)	Endings which sound like /ʃən/, spelt -tion, -sion, -ssion, -cian
Unit 11	Adding the prefix **re-**	More prefixes
Special focus 4	Homophones: *not/knot, ball/bawl, plain/plane, whether/weather, scene/seen, hear/here, week/weak, male/mail, be/bee*	Years 3 and 4 homophones
Unit 12	Adding the prefix **anti-**	More prefixes
Unit 13	Adding the prefix **super-**	More prefixes
Unit 14	Adding the prefix **sub-**	More prefixes

Read Write Inc. Spelling content matched to the National Curriculum

Practice Book 4, Log Books 3–4, Online 4

Section	Content	Link to National Curriculum requirements (English Appendix 1: Spelling)
Unit 1	Adding the prefix **mis-** and revising **un-, in-, dis-**	More prefixes
Unit 2	Words ending in *zhuh* spelt **-sure**	Words with endings sounding like /ʒə/ or /tʃə/
Special focus 1	The short *u* sound spelt **ou**: *double, trouble, enough, toughest, rougher, young, country, touch*	The /ʌ/ sound spelt ou
Unit 3	Adding the prefix **auto-**	More prefixes
Unit 4	Adding the suffix **-ly** (to adjectives to form adverbs)	The suffix -ly
Unit 5	Adding the prefix **inter-**	More prefixes
Special focus 2	Homophones: *groan/grown, main/mane, reign/rain/rein, peace/piece, berry/bury*	Years 3 and 4 homophones
Unit 6	Words with the *ay* sound spelt **ei, eigh, ey**	Words with the /eɪ/ sound spelt ei, eigh, or ey
Unit 7	Words ending in **-ous**	The suffix -ous
Unit 8	Words with the *s* sound spelt **sc**	Words with the /s/ sound spelt sc (Latin in origin)
Special focus 3	Possessive apostrophes with plural words	Possessive apostrophe with plural words
Unit 9	Words ending in *zhun* spelt **-sion**	Endings which sound like /ʒən/
Unit 10	Adding **il-** and revising **un-, in-, mis-, dis-**	More prefixes
Unit 11	The *c* sound spelt **-que** and the *g* sound spelt **-gue**	Words ending with the /g/ sound spelt -gue and the /k/ sound spelt -que (French in origin)
Special focus 4	Homophones: *heal/heel, missed/mist, who's/whose, accept/except, affect/effect*	Years 3 and 4 homophones and near-homophones
Unit 12	Adding **ir-** to words beginning with **r**	More prefixes
Unit 13	Adding the suffix **-ion** (1)	Endings which sound like /ʃən/, spelt -tion, -sion, -ssion, -cian
Unit 14	Adding the suffix **-ion** (2)	Endings which sound like /ʃən/, spelt -tion, -sion, -ssion, -cian

Read Write Inc. Spelling content matched to the National Curriculum

Practice Book 5, Log Books 5–6, Online 5

Section	Content	Link to National Curriculum requirements (English Appendix 1: Spelling)
Unit 1	Words with silent letter **b**	Words with 'silent' letters
Special focus 1	Words that contain the letter-string **ough**	Words containing the letter-string ough
Unit 2	Words ending in **-ible**	Words ending in -able and -ible
Special focus 2	Homophones	Years 5 and 6 homophones
Unit 3	Words ending in **-able**	Words ending in -able and -ible
Special focus 3	Orange words	Years 5 and 6 word list
Unit 4	Words with silent letter **t**	Words with 'silent' letters
Special focus 4	Orange words	Years 5 and 6 word list
Unit 5	Words ending in **-ibly** and **-ably**	Words ending in -ably and -ibly
Special focus 5	Homophones and other words that are easily confused	Years 5 and 6 homophones
Unit 6	Words ending in **-ent**	Words ending in -ant, -ance/-ancy, -ent, -ence/-ency
Special focus 6	Orange words	Years 5 and 6 word list
Unit 7	Words ending in **-ence**	Words ending in -ant, -ance/-ancy, -ent, -ence/-ency
Special focus 7	Orange words	Years 5 and 6 word list
Unit 8	The ee sound spelt **ei**	Words with the /i:/ sound spelt ei after c
Special focus 8	Homophones and other words that are easily confused	Years 5 and 6 homophones and other words that are often confused
Unit 9	Words ending in **-ant, -ance** and **-ancy**	Words ending in -ant, -ance/-ancy, -ent, -ence/-ency
Special focus 9	Orange words	Years 5 and 6 word list
Unit 10	Words ending in *shus* spelt **-cious**	Endings which sound like /ʃəs/ spelt -cious or -tious
Special focus 10	Orange words	Years 5 and 6 word list
Unit 11	Words ending in *shus* spelt **-tious**	Endings which sound like /ʃəs/ spelt -cious or -tious
Special focus 11	Orange words	Years 5 and 6 word list
Unit 12	Words ending in *shul* spelt **-cial** or **-tial**	Endings which sound like /ʃəl/
Special focus 12	Orange words	Years 5 and 6 word list

Read Write Inc. Spelling content matched to the National Curriculum

Practice Book 6, Log Books 5–6, Online 6

Year 6 revises key concepts from previous years, reinforcing what has already been taught.

Section	Content	Link to National Curriculum requirements (English Appendix 1: Spelling)
Unit 1	Suffixes (1)	Revising instances where we do not change the root word when a suffix beginning with a vowel is added (all years)
Special focus 1	Words containing the letter-string **ough**	Words containing the letter-string ough (Years 5 and 6)
Unit 2	Suffixes (2) (to root words ending in a consonant plus **e**)	Adding the endings -ing, -ed, -er, -est and -y to words ending in -e with a consonant before it (Year 2)
Special focus 2	Orange words	Years 5 and 6 word list
Unit 3	Suffixes (3) (to root words ending in **-le** or a consonant plus **y**)	The suffixes -ment, -ness, -ful, -less and -ly (Year 2)
Special focus 3	Homophones and other words that are easily confused	Years 5 and 6 homophones and other words that are often confused
Unit 4	Suffixes (4)	Adding suffixes beginning with vowel letters to words of more than one syllable (Years 3 and 4)
		Adding suffixes beginning with vowel letters to words ending -fer (Years 5 and 6)
Special focus 4	Orange words	Years 5 and 6 word list
Unit 5	Suffixes (5)	Adding -ed, -ing, -er and -est to a root word ending in -y with a consonant before it (Year 2)
Special focus 5	Orange words	Years 5 and 6 word list
Unit 6	The **sh** sound spelt **ti** or **ci**	Endings which sound like /ʃəs/ spelt -cious or -tious (Years 5 and 6)
Special focus 6	Homophones	Years 5 and 6 homophones
Unit 7	The **sh** sound spelt **si** or **ssi**	Endings which sound like /ʃən/ spelt -tion, -sion, -ssion, -cian (Years 3 and 4)
Special focus 7	Orange words	Years 5 and 6 word list
Unit 8	Silent letters	Words with 'silent' letters (Years 5 and 6)
Special focus 8	Orange words	Years 5 and 6 word list
Unit 9	The spellings **ei** and **ie**	Words with the /i:/ sound spelt ei after c (Years 5 and 6)
Special focus 9	Hyphens	Use of the hyphen (Years 5 and 6)
Unit 10	Words ending in **-ible** and **-able**	Words ending in -able and -ible (Years 5 and 6)
Special focus 10	Common mistakes	Homophones and other words that are often confused
Unit 11	Plural nouns (1)	Adding -es to nouns and verbs ending in -y (Year 2)
Special focus 11	Orange words	Years 5 and 6 word list
Unit 12	Plural nouns (2)	Homophones and other words that are often confused (plural nouns)
Special focus 12	Homophones and other words that are easily confused	Years 5 and 6 homophones and other words that are often confused

Assessment in *Read Write Inc. Spelling*

Assessment is an integral feature of the *Read Write Inc. Spelling* programme. All the activities involve some type of assessment, whether self, peer, group or whole-class assessment. This formative assessment is constructive, on-going monitoring for improvement, built into lively activities that children should enjoy.

Each week:

* **Speed spell** checks children's knowledge of words from the previous unit.
* **Rapid recap** checks their understanding of the new spelling concept.
* **Four-in-a-row** and **Team teach** help children assess their own spelling progress.
* **Jumping Red and Orange words** assesses children's spelling of Red/Orange words.

Practice tests

Decide entry point
In Years 3 to 6/P4 to P7, use the End of Year Practice tests on the Online Resource to decide the entry point for the spelling programme.

For example, assess Year 4/P5 using the Year 3/P4 End of Year Practice test. If they score well, start on Practice Book 3. If they find this hard, use the Year 2B End of Year Practice test.

If children share the same gaps in their spelling knowledge, only teach the necessary spelling units from an earlier year group, rather than using the whole Practice Book.

Assess half-termly
Use the Practice tests on the Online Resource every half term to assess children's progress. These use the same format as the statutory Key Stage 2 spelling tests. Each Practice test assesses 20 words taught in recent units – as well as units taught in previous year groups.

Assess at the end of each year
The End of Year Practice tests assess the spelling knowledge from the whole year, including Red and Orange words, homophones and grammar focuses.

Assessment in *Read Write Inc. Spelling*

Practice test assessment trackers

Use the Practice test assessment trackers to record and track each child's spelling progress.

	A	B	C	D	E	F	G	H	I	J	K	L	M	N	O	P	Q	R	S	T	U	V	W
1	Year 2A End of Year Practice Test																						
2	Key: Y = Year; U = Unit; S = Session (consolidation); SF = Special focus																						
3		Question number	1	2	3	4	5	6	7	8	9	10	11	12	13	14	15	16	17	18	19	20	
4	CHILD'S NAME	Test word	always	city	spotty	shiny	nearly	knight	reply	dropping	shining	energy	watch	tapped	carried	baked	would	son	people	Monday	towards	gran's	TOTAL SCORE (per child)
5		From unit	Y2AU1	Y2AU2	Y2AU3	Y2AU4	Y2AU5	Y2AU6	Y2AU7	Y2AU8	Y2AU9	Y2AU10	Y2AU11	Y2AU12	Y2AU13	Y2AU14	Y2ASF1	Y2ASF2	Y2ASF3	Y2ASF6	Y2ASF6	Y2ASF7	
6		Consolidation session	Y2AS1	Y2AS1	Y2AS2	Y2AS2	Y2AS3	Y2AS3	Y2AS4	Y2AS4	Y2AS5	Y2AS5	Y2AS6	Y2AS6	Y2AS7	Y2AS7							
7	John		✓	✓	✓	✓	✓	✓	✓	✓	✓	✓	✓	✓	✓	✓				✓	✓	✓	19
8	Lisa			✓	✓	✓	✓		✓	✓	✓	✓	✓	✓	✓	✓			✓	✓	✓	✓	15
9	Child 3																							0
10	Child 4																							0
11	Child 5																							0
12	Child 6																							0
13	Child 7																							0
14	Child 8																							0
15	Child 9																							0
16	Child 10																							0
17	Child 11																							0
18	Child 12																							0
19	Child 13																							0
20	Child 14																							0
21	Child 15																							0
22	Child 16																							0
23	Child 17																							0
24	Child 18																							0
25	Child 19																							0
26	Child 20																							0
27	Child 21																							0
28	Child 22																							0
29	Child 23																							0
30	Child 24																							0
31	Child 25																							0
32	Child 26																							0
33	Child 27																							0
34	Child 28																							0
35	Child 29																							0

Use this assessment information to regroup the children into spelling progress groups if using organisation option two or three.

Each tracker lists the words from the test so gaps in spelling knowledge can be identified for individual children, and those that are common to the whole class.

You can then teach to these gaps by revisiting the corresponding spelling unit or consolidation session.

Year 5 and 6/P6 and P7 Orange word tests

Use the half-termly Orange word tests in Year 5/P6 and Year 6/P7 to check children's knowledge of the National Curriculum word lists – that is, the word lists for Years 3/P4 and 4/P5 in Year 5/P6, and Years 5/P6 and 6/P7 in Year 6/P7.

Use the Orange word test assessment trackers to identify those words that need more practice.

Year 6/P7 Challenge Practice tests

In Year 6/P7, there are six Challenge Practice tests to assess words from Years 5/P6 and 6/P7 units only, along with more challenging words.

Using the pre-programme activities for Year 1/P2 assessment and revision

The Pre-programme activities and Practice tests can be used for assessment at the beginning of the programme. Activities 1–4 revise children's Year 1/P2 phonic knowledge and Activity 5 assesses their understanding of key concepts.

Marking spellings in children's written work

It is important that children are encouraged to write freely when they are writing their own compositions. If too much pressure is put on children to spell correctly, they will select words they know they can spell, rather than more exciting or appropriate words they cannot.

Mark children's compositions for the quality of ideas and use of language. These comments should be discussed with children before looking at punctuation and spelling.

- ✯ Underline, lightly, in pencil, common errors that children will be likely to correct quickly without a dictionary.

- ✯ Underline, more heavily, repeated errors which you really want them to spell correctly.

- ✯ Put a wavy line under exciting words and, if spelt incorrectly, write the correct spelling lightly in pencil, praising children for having made such a fabulous attempt at an adventurous word! Do not ask them to correct it themselves by looking in a dictionary – you may put them off using ambitious words.

Keep your own log of common errors. Make a mark against misspelt words that have been taught in the spelling lesson, to remind you to review the unit.

The statutory end of Key Stage tests

Following the *Read Write Inc. Spelling* programme will help to prepare children for the spelling component of the English grammar, punctuation and spelling tests at the end of Key Stage 1 and Key Stage 2.

The tests will draw on the range of strategies and morphological awareness specified in the statutory spelling appendix to the National Curriculum in England, all of which are covered by *Read Write Inc. Spelling*. The tests may include words drawn from the word lists in the National Curriculum (covered by the Red and Orange words in this programme), but will not be limited to them.

Assessment in *Read Write Inc. Spelling*

How can I prepare children for the tests?

All the spelling skills and knowledge required for the statutory tests are embedded in the teaching and learning of the *Read Write Inc. Spelling* programme. They are covered in a variety of ways:

- The Pre-programme activities and Year 1 Practice tests can be used to assess children's phonic knowledge as well as their understanding of the key spelling concepts taught in Year 1 of the National Curriculum in England.

- The units and Special focus sessions cover all the spelling requirements of the National Curriculum in England.

- The words in the Word banks can be used for a variety of learning and revision purposes (see 'Activities for teaching Red and Orange words' on pp.41–43).

- Consolidation sessions can be used to reinforce learning.

- Spelling Log Books give children a sense of ownership over their own learning, and are useful records of progress.

- Red and Orange words are frequently discussed and practised through engaging, fun activities.

- Year 6 revises all previous years' learning, reinforcing and refreshing what has previously been taught. (See overview of content on p.50.)

- Practice tests are provided online. There is one for each term in every year group of the programme (plus two for Year 1 and six extra Challenge tests for Year 6). These tests can be conducted in the same manner as the statutory tests, in order to familiarize children with the procedure.

The National Curriculum in England

Detailed coverage of English Appendix 1: Spelling is shown on pp.44–50. These tables summarize coverage of spelling content from the main Programmes of study (Writing – transcription) for the National Curriculum in England.

Year 2

Link to National Curriculum requirements (Programme of study: Writing – transcription)	*Read Write Inc. Spelling* programme content
Pupils should be taught to:	
• spell by: • segmenting spoken words into phonemes and representing these by graphemes, spelling many correctly	Throughout programme
• learning new ways of spelling phonemes for which one or more spellings are already known, and learn some words with each spelling, including a few common homophones	Throughout programme
• learning to spell common exception words	Online Word banks Jumping Red words – every unit
• learning to spell more words with contracted forms	*Practice Book 2A* Special focus 5: Contractions and apostrophes (p.40) *Practice Book 2B* Special focus 6: Contractions and apostrophes (p.43)
• learning the possessive apostrophe (singular) [for example, the girl's book]	*Practice Book 2A* Special focus 7: Possessive apostrophes (p.54) *Practice Book 2B* Special focus 7: Possessive apostrophes (p.53)
• distinguishing between homophones and near-homophones	*Practice Book 2A* Special focus 2: Homophones (p.19)
• add suffixes to spell longer words, including -ment, -ness, -ful, -less, -ly	*Practice Book 2B* Unit 13: Adding the suffix -ment (p.44) *Practice Book 2B* Unit 6: Adding the suffix -ness 1 (p.19) and Adding the suffix -ness 2 (p.23) *Practice Book 2B* Unit 11: Adding the suffix -ful (p.37) *Practice Book 2B* Unit 12: Adding the suffix -less (p.40) *Practice Book 2A* Unit 5: Adding the suffix -ly (p.20)
• apply spelling rules and guidance, as listed in English Appendix 1	See charts on pp.44–46
• write from memory simple sentences dictated by the teacher that include words using the GPCs, common exception words and punctuation taught so far.	Dictation activity – throughout programme

The National Curriculum in England

Years 3 and 4

Link to National Curriculum requirements (Programme of study: Writing – transcription)	*Read Write Inc. Spelling* programme content
Pupils should be taught to:	
• use further prefixes and suffixes and understand how to add them (English Appendix 1)	See charts on pp.47-48
• spell further homophones	*Practice Book 3* Special focus 2: Homophones (p.23) *Practice Book 3* Special focus 4: Homophones (p.49) *Practice Book 4* Special focus 2: Homophones (p.23) *Practice Book 4* Special focus 4: Homophones (p.49)
• spell words that are often misspelt (English Appendix 1)	Throughout programme Online Word banks (Orange words are word list words) Jumping Orange words – every unit
• place the possessive apostrophe accurately in words with regular plurals [for example, girls', boys'] and in words with irregular plurals [for example, children's]	*Practice Book 4* Special focus 3: Possessive apostrophes with plural words (p.36)
• use the first two or three letters of a word to check its spelling in a dictionary	Dictionary challenge activities: *Practice Book 3* p.16 and p.29 and *Practice Book 4* p.20 and p.51
• write from memory simple sentences, dictated by the teacher, that include words and punctuation taught so far.	Dictation activity – throughout programme

Years 5 and 6

Link to National Curriculum requirements (Programme of study: Writing – transcription)	*Read Write Inc. Spelling* programme content
Pupils should be taught to:	
• use further prefixes and suffixes and understand the guidance for adding them	See charts on pp.49-50
• spell some words with 'silent' letters [for example, knight, psalm, solemn]	*Practice Book 5* Unit 1: Words with silent letter b (p.2) *Practice Book 5* Unit 4: Words with silent letter t (p.17) *Practice Book 6* Unit 8: Silent letters (p.37)
• continue to distinguish between homophones and other words which are often confused	*Practice Book 5* Special focus 2: Homophones (p.11) *Practice Book 5* Special focus 5: Homophones and other words that are easily confused (p.26) *Practice Book 5* Special focus 8: Homophones and other words that are easily confused (p.41) *Practice Book 6* Special focus 3: Homophones and other words that are often confused (p.16) *Practice Book 6* Special focus 6: Homophones and other words that are often confused (p.31) *Practice Book 6* Special focus 10: Common mistakes (p.51) *Practice Book 6* Special focus 12: Homophones and other words that are often confused (p.61)
• use knowledge of morphology and etymology in spelling and understand that the spelling of some words needs to be learnt specifically, as listed in English Appendix 1	See charts on pp.49-50
• use dictionaries to check the spelling and meaning of words	Dictionary challenge activities: *Practice Book 5* p.3 and p.48 and *Practice Book 6* p.2, p.31, p.46 and p.58
• use the first three or four letters of a word to check spelling, meaning or both of these in a dictionary	Dictionary challenge activities: *Practice Book 5* p.3 and p.48 and *Practice Book 6* p.2, p.31, p.46 and p.58
• use a thesaurus.	Thesaurus challenge activities: *Practice Book 5* p.17, p.22, p.43 and p.58 and *Practice Book 6* p.8, p.23, p.28, p.33 and p.38

Scotland: Curriculum for Excellence

Read Write Inc. Spelling uses a proven approach underpinned by phonics to teach spelling to children in Primary 3–7 who are fluent readers. Throughout the programme, children are taught strategies to enable them to spell accurately, including understanding morphology and etymology, plus building and consolidating their knowledge of frequently misspelt words, exception words, tricky homophones and other words that are easily confused. The approach is structured and cumulative, building children's accuracy and confidence year by year.

For a detailed outline of the spelling concepts covered in each unit of *Read Write Inc. Spelling*, please see pp.44–50.

Year group	Primary 3	Primary 4	Primary 5	Primary 6	Primary 7
	Read Write Inc. Spelling starts here				
Read Write Inc. Spelling resources (Handbook covers all years)	Practice Books 2A and 2B Log Book 2 Online 2	Practice Book 3 Log Book 3–4 Online 3–4	Practice Book 4 Log Book 3–4 Online 3–4	Practice Book 5 Log Book 5–6 Online 5–6	Practice Book 6 Log Book 5–6 Online 5–6
Scotland Curriculum for Excellence levels Note: this level guidance is approximate	**First** **Writing – Tools for writing** • using knowledge of technical aspects to help my writing communicate effectively within and beyond my place of learning *I can spell the most commonly-used words, using my knowledge of letter patterns and spelling rules and use resources to help me spell tricky or unfamiliar words.* **LIT 1–21a**			**Second** **Writing – Tools for writing** • using knowledge of technical aspects to help my writing communicate effectively within and beyond my place of learning *I can spell most of the words I need to communicate, using spelling rules, specialist vocabulary, self-correction techniques and a range of resources.* **LIT 2–21a** (Continuing to Third: *I can use a range of strategies and resources and spell most of the words I need to use, including specialist vocabulary, and ensure that my spelling is accurate.* **LIT 3–21a**)	

Wales: Curriculum for Wales Framework

Read Write Inc. Spelling uses a proven approach underpinned by phonics to teach spelling to children in Years 2–6 who are fluent readers. Throughout the programme, children are taught strategies to enable them to spell accurately, including understanding morphology and etymology, plus building and consolidating their knowledge of frequently misspelt words, exception words, tricky homophones and other words that are easily confused. The approach is structured and cumulative, building children's accuracy and confidence year by year.

For a detailed outline of the spelling concepts covered in each unit of *Read Write Inc. Spelling*, please see pp.44–50.

Year group	Year 2 Progression Step 2	Year 3 Progression Step 2	Year 4 Progression Step 3	Year 5 Progression Step 3	Year 6 Progression Step 3
Read Write Inc. Spelling resources (Handbook covers all years)	*Read Write Inc. Spelling* starts here Practice Books 2A and 2B Log Book 2 Online 2	Practice Book 3 Log Book 3–4 Online 3–4	Practice Book 4 Log Book 3–4 Online 3–4	Practice Book 5 Log Book 5–6 Online 5–6	Practice Book 6 Log Book 5–6 Online 5–6
Descriptions of Learning	Learners are able to: • spell common irregular words correctly • use knowledge of letter sounds and patterns accurately in spelling • attempt to spell more difficult words plausibly using a range of strategies • spell high-frequency words correctly • use knowledge of letter sounds and patterns to support spelling.	Learners are able to: • spell common irregular words correctly • use knowledge of letter sounds and patterns accurately in spelling • attempt to spell more difficult words plausibly using a range of strategies • spell high-frequency words correctly • use knowledge of letter sounds and patterns to support spelling.	Learners are able to: • attempt to spell more difficult words plausibly using a range of strategies.	Learners are able to: • attempt to spell more difficult words plausibly using a range of strategies.	Learners are able to: • attempt to spell more difficult words plausibly using a range of strategies.

© Oxford University Press 2023. This page may be reproduced for use solely within the purchaser's school or college.

Northern Ireland: Levels of progression in Communication across the curriculum

Northern Ireland: Levels of progression in Communication across the curriculum: Primary (Levels 1–5)

Read Write Inc. Spelling uses a proven approach underpinned by phonics to teach spelling to children in Primary 3–7 who are fluent readers. Throughout the programme, children are taught strategies to enable them to spell accurately, including understanding morphology and etymology, plus building and consolidating their knowledge of frequently misspelt words, exception words, tricky homophones and other words that are easily confused. The approach is structured and cumulative, building children's accuracy and confidence year by year.

For a detailed outline of the spelling concepts covered in each unit of *Read Write Inc. Spelling*, please see pp.44–50.

Year group	P3	P4	P5	P6	P7
Read Write Inc. Spelling resources (Handbook covers all years)	*Read Write Inc. Spelling* starts here Practice Books 2A and 2B Log Book 2 Online 2	Practice Book 3 Log Book 3–4 Online 3–4	Practice Book 4 Log Book 3–4 Online 3–4	Practice Book 5 Log Book 5–6 Online 5–6	Practice Book 6 Log Book 5–6 Online 5–6
	Key Stage 1 Pupils are expected to reach Level 2 by the end of Key Stage 1. There is also an expectation that they will progress by at least one level between each Key Stage.		**Key Stage 2** Pupils are expected to reach Level 4 by the end of Key Stage 2. There is also an expectation that they will progress by at least one level between each Key Stage.		
	Level 1/2	Level 2	Level 3	Level 4	Level 4/5
Levels of progression in Communication across the curriculum: Primary (Levels 1–5) • talk about, plan and edit work • write with increasing accuracy and proficiency.	**Pupils can:** (Level 1) write words using sound-symbol correspondence • (Level 1) write personal and familiar words. **In a limited and specified range of forms, pupils can:** • (Level 2) spell and write common and familiar words recognizably.	**In a range of forms, for different audiences and purposes, pupils can:** • (Level 2) spell and write common and familiar words recognizably.	**In a range of specified forms and for specified audiences and purposes, pupils can:** • (Level 3) make improvements to their writing • (Level 3) spell and write frequently used and topic words correctly.	**In a range of forms, for different audiences and purposes, pupils can:** • (Level 4) check writing to make improvements in accuracy and meaning • (Level 4) use accurate grammar and spelling on most occasions.	**In a range of forms, for different audiences and purposes, including in formal situations, pupils can:** • (Level 5) redraft to improve accuracy and meaning • (Level 5) use accurate grammar and spelling.

© Oxford University Press 2023. This page may be reproduced for use solely within the purchaser's school or college.

Northern Ireland: Key Stages 1 and 2 Areas of Learning – Language and Literacy

Year group	P3	P4	P5	P6	P7
Read Write Inc. Spelling resources (Handbook covers all years)	*Practice Books 2A and 2B* *Log Book 2* *Online 2*	*Practice Book 3* *Log Book 3–4* *Online 3–4*	*Practice Book 4* *Log Book 3–4* *Online 3–4*	*Practice Book 5* *Log Book 5–6* *Online 5–6*	*Practice Book 6* *Log Book 5–6* *Online 5–6*
	Key Stage 1 Pupils are expected to reach Level 2 by the end of Key Stage 1. There is also an expectation that they will progress by at least one level between each Key Stage.		**Key Stage 2** Pupils are expected to reach Level 4 by the end of Key Stage 2. There is also an expectation that they will progress by at least one level between each Key Stage.		
Language and Literacy	**Writing** Children should be enabled to: • use a variety of skills to spell words in their writing • spell correctly a range of familiar, important and regularly occurring words.		**Writing** Children should be enabled to: • use a variety of skills to spell words correctly.		

Overview of activities on the Extra Practice Zone

The Extra Practice Zone has more than 1000 activity pages, providing further practice and consolidation for faster progress. It is available on the Read Write Inc. Spelling Online Resource on Oxford Owl for School. For an overview of the Extra Practice Zone, please see pp.10–11. Here is an overview of the activities on the Extra Practice Zone.

1. **Spell the Vowel**
   This keying-in gap-fill activity provides practice in spelling words with the following vowel sounds: a, e, i, o, u, ay, ee, igh, ow, oo, oo, ar, or, air, ir, ou, oy, ire, ear, ure.

2. **Sounds the Same**
   This drag-and-drop gap-fill activity provides practice in using the correct spelling of a homophone or near-homophone in context.

3. **Swap, Double or Drop?**
   This multiple-choice activity provides practice in identifying how the spelling of a root word changes when a suffix is added.

4. **Rule Breakers**
   This multiple-choice activity provides practice in the spelling rules and reminds children that there are exceptions to these rules.

5. **Playing with Plurals**
   This keying-in gap-fill activity provides practice in spelling singular and plural forms of nouns.

Overview of activities on the Extra Practice Zone

6. Word Endings
This dropdown gap-fill activity provides practice in spelling words with the following word endings: ant/ent, ance/ence, ancy/ency, able/ible, ably/ibly, cial/tial, el/al/il.

7. Silent Letters
Years 5 and 6/P6 and 7 only. This highlighting activity provides practice in identifying silent letters within words.

8. Spell the Root
This drag-and-drop gap-fill activity provides practice in identifying and spelling root words for words with prefixes and suffixes.

9. Odd Sound Out
This multiple-choice activity provides practice in identifying graphemes and words that originate from other languages (Greek, French or Latin in origin).

10. Odd Rhyme Out
Years 3–6/P4–7 only. This multiple-choice activity provides practice in identifying words that rhyme.

OXFORD
UNIVERSITY PRESS

Great Clarendon Street, Oxford, OX2 6DP, United Kingdom

Oxford University Press is a department of the University of Oxford.
It furthers the University's objective of excellence in research, scholarship,
and education by publishing worldwide. Oxford is a registered trade mark
of Oxford University Press in the UK and in certain other countries

© Oxford University Press 2023

The moral rights of the authors have been asserted

First Edition published in 2014

This Edition published in 2023

All rights reserved. No part of this publication may be reproduced, stored in a retrieval system, or transmitted, in any form or by any means, without the prior permission in writing of Oxford University Press, or as expressly permitted by law, by licence or under terms agreed with the appropriate reprographics rights organization. Enquiries concerning reproduction outside the scope of the above should be sent to the Rights Department, Oxford University Press, at the address above.

You must not circulate this work in any other form
and you must impose this same condition on any acquirer

British Library Cataloguing in Publication Data

Data available

ISBN: 978-1-38-204046-4

1 3 5 7 9 10 8 6 4 2

Paper used in the production of this book is a natural, recyclable product made from wood grown in sustainable forests. The manufacturing process conforms to the environmental regulations of the country of origin.

Printed in Great Britain by Ashford Colour Press, Gosport, Hants

Acknowledgements

Illustrations by Andrés Martínez Ricci and Kate Sheppard

Cover illustration by Andrés Martínez Ricci

Oxford OWL

For teachers
Helping you with free eBooks, inspirational resources, advice and support

For parents
Helping your child's learning with free eBooks, essential tips and fun activities

www.oxfordowl.co.uk